PITCHWORTHY

WHAT PEOPLE ARE SAYING ABOUT
PITCHWORTHY

"KJ entered my business journey at a time when I felt overwhelmed and unsure how to articulate what made our brand special. She helped me not only find the words but find my confidence again. Her PR coaching felt like sitting down with a friend who just gets it—someone who sees your vision and knows exactly how to help the world see it too. Working with her was the push I didn't know I needed, and I'll forever be grateful for the clarity and momentum she gave me."

— Jessica Hannesson, Founder of Hannesson Home Interiors

"KJ is equal parts PR wizard and brand cheerleader. She takes big, overwhelming tasks and turns them into simple, bite-sized successes. Thanks to her, Joy Creative Shop has been featured in numerous publications and media outlets—all while keeping the process fun and helping us stay true to our authentic values."

— Steph Weibring, Founder of Joy Creative Shop

"Before working with KJ, our interior design firm was struggling to stand out in a crowded market. Her strategic approach and relentless drive transformed our visibility completely. Now we're consistently featured in top publications and have a waitlist of high-end clients. KJ's humble yet resourceful approach keeps making us more successful every month."

— Laura McCroskey, Founder of McCroskey Interiors

"Since 2019, KJ has been the strategic partner I can trust with every part of my brand. She has the rare gift of taking the complexity of who you are—your story, your goals, your future—and shaping it into messaging that connects. She's been my cheerleader, my pep-talk giver, and my behind-the-scenes powerhouse who delivers work with speed, brilliance, and heart. Thanks to KJ, I've had seamless continuity across media pitches, website copy, social content, and press placements, and more importantly, the confidence to step fully into my vision knowing I had her in my corner."

— Maegan Lujan,
Director of Solutions and Services Marketing at Toshiba

"In an oversaturated marketplace, KJ doesn't just help you stand out, she makes sure you rise above. Her insight is razor-sharp, her connections far-reaching, and her ability to balance big-picture vision with tactical detail makes her an invaluable partner. She knows how to get the right people talking about you and why it matters."

— Casey Brown,
Founder and Director of Necker Island Pickleball Forum & Pro-Am

PITCHWORTHY

THE NO-FLUFF PLAYBOOK
TO PUBLICITY THAT PAYS OFF

KJ BLATTENBAUER

Publishing support provided by
Ignite Press
55 Shaw Ave. Suite 204
Clovis, CA 93612
www.IgnitePress.us

ISBN: 979-8-9932676-0-9
ISBN: 979-8-9932676-1-6 (E-book)

For bulk purchases and for booking, contact:

KJ Blattenbauer
hello@hearsaypr.com
www.hearsaypr.com

Library of Congress Control Number: 2025925883

Cover design by Usman Tariq
Edited by Cathy Cruise
Interior design by Jetlaunch

FIRST EDITION

To KB—my greatest support, loudest cheerleader, and ultimate hype man. I wouldn't dream half as big without you in my corner.

Table of Contents

Letter to My Reader

Hello, friend!

Consider this your official invitation to step into the spotlight.

You've built something real. Something powerful.

Now it's time to make sure the right people see it, talk about it, and *can't stop coming back for more.*

This isn't just Public Relations 101.

This is the evolution of everything I've learned in nearly three decades of being an award-winning publicist helping brands and businesses go from best-kept secret to go-to source.

You've seen others get the bylines. You've watched others lead successful launches. You've probably even shared their links.

But now? It's about getting *you* featured.

It's about making you Pitchworthy—and keeping you that way.

This book isn't a list of hacks or one-size-fits-all tips.

It's a roadmap for visibility that feels aligned, sustainable, and wildly effective.

It's about building buzz *and* a business. Press *and* positioning. Impact *and* income.

And if you've ever felt like you were meant to be known—really known—for your ideas, your work, and your vision?

You're in the right place.

By the end of this book, you won't just feel confident pitching yourself.

You'll learn how to become magnetic to the media and impossible to overlook.

Let's get started.

– KJ

CHAPTER 1

What Is PR?

Let's get one thing straight: public relations isn't about making noise. It's about making meaning.

At its core, PR is the art (and strategy) of getting someone outside your usual circle to care. To amplify your message, advocate for your mission, and help position you as the go-to voice in your field.

PR isn't just press, it's how you control the conversation about you.

When done well, PR builds your reputation, boosts your credibility, and places you—and your ideas—into the kinds of conversations that move markets and shape narratives.

It's not just about getting attention. It's about becoming Pitchworthy, and staying that way.

Forget Everything You Think You Know About PR

PR isn't just about press.

It's not a Hail Mary pitch. It's not a perfectly filtered post. And it's definitely not paying to play.

Public relations is earned attention. It's third-party validation from someone whose opinion holds weight. Think newspapers, magazines, podcasts, blogs, TV segments, speaking stages, and yes, even the DMs of that influencer who actually moves product.

It's what happens when someone *else* says, "This is worth knowing about."

PR gives you something money can't buy: *trust*.

What PR Actually Looks Like

PR shows up in many forms, and the best brands use it across the board.

Think:

- Strategic media pitches that land you in the headlines your audience actually reads
- Announcements that promote your next big move to the right outlets
- Interviews, guest spots, and event appearances that position you as a leader
- Influencer and affiliate relationships that bring your brand into new circles
- Original thought leadership (blogs, op-eds, columns) that showcase your expertise
- Social media with purpose, not just for the algorithm but for amplification

When aligned under one cohesive message, these efforts work in tandem to grow your visibility, nurture your audience, and convert attention into opportunity.

PR, when done right, creates *momentum*.

Why PR Works

Let's be honest: We don't trust ads. We trust people.

We trust recommendations, reviews, and reputations.

And most of today's purchasing decisions? They're influenced long before the "add to cart" moment.

Think about the last thing you invested in, whether it's a business coach, a bag, or a dinner reservation. You likely checked the website, asked around, skimmed testimonials, maybe even spotted the brand in a magazine or online feature. That social proof? That's PR at work.

PR doesn't just inform. It persuades. It positions. It builds authority at scale.

Is PR Worth It? Let's Look at the Math

Still wondering if PR is worth your time?

- Full-page ad in a regional newspaper: ~$3,000
- Full-page ad in a national publication: $75,000+
- Hiring a PR agency: $2,500 to $20,000 per month
- Securing press coverage on your own: $0

And here's the kicker: Earned media (coverage you don't pay for) has 7x the credibility of traditional advertising. Why? Because someone else is vouching for you. Not you selling you.

What If You've Never Pitched Before?

Here's the part they don't tell you: PR isn't rocket science. It's relationship-building. It's consistency. It's clarity.

And no one, not even the best publicist, knows your story better than you do.

If you can dedicate an hour or two a week, do a little research, and send a few bold, well-crafted emails, you can get press. Not some-day. Now.

Here's what this book will show you:

- How to pitch yourself with confidence
- How to craft a story the media actually wants
- How to build a reputation that goes beyond one moment in the spotlight

You don't need a million followers, a fancy PR agency, or a viral hook. You just need a smart strategy, a clear message, and the belief that you are already worthy of being seen.

Because you are.

You're not just PR-ready. You're Pitchworthy.

Pitchworthy Power Move

Position yourself before you pitch yourself.

Before you send a single email, ask: *What do I want to be known for?* When your message is clear, every PR opportunity becomes a spotlight, *not* a guessing game.

Pro tip: One specific, compelling angle will land more coverage than 10 vague ones.

PR Myth You Can Ditch

"You're not ready for PR yet."

Wrong.

You don't need a huge following, a perfect website, or a big launch to start.

You just need a point of view and the courage to back it up.

Visibility isn't a reward for success. It's how you build it.

Pitchworthy Prompt

When your name comes up in conversation, what do you want people to say?

Now ask yourself, does your current visibility reflect that?

CHAPTER 2

Targeting Your Target Audience

Let's be honest. Most brands don't fail because they're not good.
They fail because they're invisible to the people who would care.
Visibility without intentionality is noise.

And PR without a clear audience? That's just expensive guessing.

Before you can pitch anyone, you have to understand who you're pitching for.

Not *in theory*. Not *in hopes*. In reality.

This chapter is where we refine the foundation. You'll walk away with a crystal-clear picture of who your work is meant to reach, and how to find them, talk to them, and make them care.

Without a clear audience, your pitch is just noise.

Because contrary to what hustle culture would have you believe, *your audience is not everyone*. And trying to market to everyone is the fastest way to be remembered by no one.

The Problem Isn't Your Pitch. It's Your Positioning.

I can't tell you how many smart, driven founders I meet who say, "I just want more clients," or "I want to grow my audience," but haven't taken the time to define who that audience actually is.

Not a vague ideal client avatar. Not a Pinterest mood board.

I'm talking real-world clarity:

- Who are they?
- What do they need?
- Where do they spend time?
- And why should they care *right now*?

That's your job to know—not the media's, not the market's.

You can't position yourself as the go-to if you don't know who you're speaking to.

Who's Your Audience, Really?

Let's break it down. Your target audience is the group of people who will benefit most from what you offer. Not who could *technically* use it, but who's actively looking for a solution, hungry for expertise, or ready to invest.

If you're already in business, look at your best clients.

Who said yes quickly? Who got the best results? Who sent referrals?

If you're new, research your competitors. Not to copy, but to identify the gaps they're leaving wide open. Those gaps? That's where you show up.

And please, *don't* make assumptions. Just because you love your brand doesn't mean your audience understands why it matters. You've got to bridge that gap through research, listening, and data.

Your Audience Isn't Static. It's Strategic.

Audience clarity isn't a one-and-done exercise. As your brand grows, your audience may shift. You may expand your offerings. Launch something new. Enter new markets.

The real question isn't just, *Who's my audience now?* It's:

- *Who do I want to attract?*
- *Who is already paying attention?*
- *And how can I refine my visibility to serve both?*

PR is precision work. And the sharper your audience profile, the better your chances of landing in the places that matter to them.

Demographics Are a Start.
But Psychographics Seal the Deal.

Sure, you need to know their age, income, and zip code.
   But if you want to resonate, you need to go deeper.
   Get curious about:

- What do they value?
- What keeps them up at night?
- What influences their decisions?
- What kinds of stories do they click on and share?

The more clearly you understand how your audience *thinks and behaves*, the more magnetic your messaging becomes.

Know Who You're Competing With—
and Where You Win

Studying your competitors is not about playing copycat. It's about identifying whitespace.

   Ask:

- What are their customers raving about?
- What are they frustrated by?
- Where do their offerings fall short?

Find the gap.
Then own it.
That's how brands carve out not just audience share, but attention.

Want Real Data? Go to the Source.

Research tools like Google Trends, Quantcast, and Similarweb can give you a sense of market behavior. But primary research is where the gold lives.

Interview your audience. Run surveys. Start conversations.

Listen to how they talk about their problems, not how you describe your solution.

When you speak your audience's language, PR becomes less about persuasion and more about resonance.

Your Target Audience Is the Gateway to Visibility

Once you know exactly who you're trying to reach, the rest becomes simpler.

Pitching gets easier. Media opportunities become more aligned.

Messaging sharpens. Offers convert.

You stop guessing.

You start connecting.

That's how visibility becomes inevitable.

The truth? PR isn't about luck, timing, or who you know. It's about what you're brave enough to say—and how often you're willing to say it.

Pitchworthy Power Move

Clarity beats charisma.

You don't need to be louder. You need to be more specific. Define your audience so precisely that people recognize themselves the second they land on your page or see your name in a headline.

PR Myth You Can Ditch

"You don't want to niche down. You'll lose people."

False.

Broad messages blur. Specific ones convert. The more clearly you define who you're for, the more magnetic you become.

Pitchworthy Prompt

What does your audience believe about their problem, and how do you challenge or reinforce that belief?

Understanding what they already think is the key to shaping what they do next.

CHAPTER 3

Setting PR Goals

I f you want to become known, not just noticed, you need to start with intention.

Because in PR—just like in business—visibility without strategy is noise.

If you can't measure it, you can't make it matter.

The fastest way to waste time pitching, posting, or praying for press is to skip this step.

Let's fix that now.

The Power of Purpose in PR

Your PR goals shape everything: what you pitch, who you pitch to, when you pitch it, and how you follow through.

A good goal acts like a North Star. It anchors your strategy and filters your decisions. Without it, you're just chasing features for the sake of feeling "seen." And that's not the kind of attention that lasts.

Before you send another email or post a "press hit" graphic, let's take a step back and ask:

- *Why do I want visibility in the first place?*
- *What do I want PR to do for my business?*
- *How will I measure success that isn't just tied to sales?*

Because while PR can absolutely grow your audience and revenue, it does so *indirectly*. It builds credibility, creates momentum, and fuels trust, which makes your marketing and sales work 10x better.

But that only happens when you set clear, aligned goals upfront.

Start with "Why"

Let's get practical. Before you begin pitching, ask yourself:

- *Why am I doing this?*
- *What do I hope this visibility will lead to?*

Be honest with yourself. There are no wrong answers, but there *are* vague ones. "Get more exposure" isn't enough.

Instead, think:

- *Do I want to increase email subscribers by 20 percent in the next quarter?*
- *Am I hoping to land a TEDx talk or conference invite?*
- *Do I want more inbound leads from qualified buyers?*
- *Is my goal to shift how people perceive me in my industry?*

Those are real goals. Tangible. Measurable. Motivating.

Know the Difference: Goals Versus Strategies

A common mistake? Confusing what you're *doing* with what you're aiming *to achieve*.

Getting featured in *Forbes* isn't a PR goal. That's a strategy.

The goal might be:

- To be seen as a thought leader in the startup space
- To earn credibility that accelerates investor trust
- To grow your waitlist before a product launch

You need all. But you must know which is which.

Define What's Valuable (Beyond Sales)

Public relations isn't advertising, and its ROI doesn't always show up as a dollar sign.

Studies show PR typically accounts for five to seven percent of sales impact, but that doesn't mean it's not worth the investment. In fact, PR often makes your *other* efforts—like launches, email campaigns, and social selling—more effective.

When setting PR goals, consider value beyond the bottom line:

- Website metrics: Are you seeing more traffic? Better engagement?
- Social proof: Is your audience talking about you more? Are you being shared or tagged organically?
- Reputation lift: Are people perceiving you differently after your visibility grows?
- Inbound opportunities: Are podcasters, event coordinators, or clients reaching out because they "saw you in something"?

The more specific you are, the easier it is to track momentum.

Get Analytical (Yes, Even in PR)

Just like social media and marketing, PR is trackable if you know what to look for.

Here's what you should pay attention to:

- Impressions and mentions: How often is your name being picked up, shared, or quoted?
- Traffic sources: Where are your clicks coming from? Can you tie spikes to specific press features?
- SEO lift: Are more people searching for your name or brand after a media hit?
- Lead behavior: Are media features shortening your sales cycle or improving conversion?

You can also measure things like bounce rate, time on site, and which features lead to new subscribers or customer inquiries.

Pro tip: Add "How did you hear about us?" to your forms and DMs. It's simple, but powerful.

Positioning Matters

Part of goal-setting is understanding *how* you want to be perceived. Ask yourself:

- Do I want to be seen as a disruptor? A trusted expert? A luxury brand?
- Am I being quoted as a go-to authority in my niche? Or am I still introducing myself from scratch?
- Are media outlets coming to *me* yet?

These questions help you shape your brand's *positioning* goals. Because remember, *who* you are in the media matters just as much as where you show up.

The PR Goals That Actually Move the Needle

Need inspiration? Here are four smart, common PR goals—and how they work in real life:

1. Promote Goodwill

   Want to show that you're a brand with heart and purpose? Participate in charitable programs, spotlight your community impact, or align with values-based organizations. This builds long-term loyalty, not just short-term buzz.

2. Raise Awareness

   This is the goal for new brands, for product launches, or when entering a new market. Think campaign-driven outreach, event PR, or podcast blitzes tied to timely angles. Awareness campaigns make sure people *know* you exist, and remember why.

3. Shift Perception

    If you're elevating your brand or moving into new territory, PR helps reintroduce you. Want to go from scrappy solopreneur to trusted advisor? That's a positioning shift. From "underdog" to "undeniable"? That's what PR does best.

4. Educate and Inform

    If your product or service needs explanation or myth-busting, this is your move. Show up where your audience learns—industry blogs, guest essays, tutorials, trend reports—and make your voice the one they trust.

Put Your Goals to Work

Once your goals are defined, your PR strategy becomes much easier to build.

Every pitch has a purpose. Every placement moves the needle. Every opportunity is filtered through the lens of *why* you're doing it.

And that? That's how you go from chasing attention to owning it.

Pitchworthy Power Move

Start every pitch with your end game in mind.

Ask: *If this lands, what happens next?* PR with purpose leads to outcomes you can measure, and momentum you can replicate.

PR Myth You Can Ditch

"You want to get featured everywhere."

You don't need *everywhere*. You need the *right* places. Media coverage isn't the finish line. It's the leverage point.

Pitchworthy Prompt

If you got your dream media placement tomorrow, what business result would make it worth it?

Now back into your strategy from there.

CHAPTER 4

Brainstorming Brand Words

Let's talk about something most people skip, but that no truly Pitchworthy brand can afford to overlook: the *words* that define who you are.

Not your elevator pitch. Not your value proposition. The *language* that captures your essence.

The vocabulary of your visibility starts with your brand words.

Your brand words aren't copy. They're character. They set the tone, shape the perception, and build the emotional bridge between your brilliance and the audience meant for it.

Get them right, and every headline, pitch, caption, and campaign becomes instantly more magnetic.

Get them wrong—or worse, vague—and everything starts to blend in. Including you.

Why Brand Words Matter (More Than You Think)

Over the past 28+ years, I've watched founders obsess over logos, colors, and taglines, yet struggle to explain *who* they are and *how* they want their audience to feel. That's where brand words come in.

They aren't fluff. They're function.

Think of your brand words as your PR compass. They:

- Guide your messaging
- Shape your tone
- Help you show up consistently across platforms
- Create alignment between how you *see* your brand and how others *experience* it

Most importantly, they help you communicate from a place of clarity, not just creativity. Because clarity is what turns attention into traction.

What Brand Words Actually Are

Brand words are three to five intentional adjectives or short phrases that reflect how your audience should feel about your brand, and how you want to be perceived in the public eye.

They're not your personal values (though those influence them). They're not your aesthetic (though they inform it). They're your *emotional signature*.

Let's say you run a luxury floral design studio. Your brand words might be:

- Elevated
- Wildly romantic
- Intentional
- Rooted

A wellness coach? You might go with:

- Grounded
- Empowering
- Transformational
- Sacred

A PR agency (hi, Hearsay)?

- Strategic
- Sophisticated

- Bold
- Energetic

Now picture those words on your homepage, in a magazine feature, or as the inspiration for your social captions. Suddenly, your brand starts feeling cohesive, confident, and *alive*.

Where Brand Words Show Up

Once you define them, your brand words become your shorthand. You'll use them to:

- Craft stronger media pitches
- Choose which publications and platforms align with your voice
- Write captions that feel like *you*, not a content calendar robot
- Approve design, visuals, and collaborations that actually match your vibe
- Gut-check future team members, clients, or partnerships for brand fit

In short, they're the foundation of how your brand speaks, and how the world speaks *about* you.

How to Choose Your Brand Words

This isn't a color quiz or personality test. There's no filter. No gimmick. This process takes real reflection, and a willingness to own your voice with precision.

Let's break it down into five phases.

Phase One: Know Your Audience's Emotional State

Start by asking:

- *What's my audience feeling* before *they come into contact with my brand?*
- *What challenges are they facing?*

- *What questions are they asking themselves?*
- *What do they hope I can offer?*

This helps ground your brand voice in empathy, not ego. Your audience is the mirror you reflect in your messaging.

Example: If your audience is burned out creatives seeking inspiration, words like "restorative," "liberating," or "soulful" might show up on your list.

If they're growth-stage CEOs in high-stakes roles, you might lean toward "decisive," "authoritative," or "streamlined."

Phase Two: Define the Desired Experience

Next, ask:

- *What should interacting with my brand* feel *like?*
- *When someone visits my website, joins my community, or reads my article, what energy do I want to leave them with?*

List out adjectives that describe the *emotional result* you want to create. If you're a brand strategist, maybe your words are "sharp," "insightful," and "clarifying." If you sell handmade ceramics, maybe it's "calm," "intentional," and "earthy."

Don't just think pretty. Think precise.

Phase Three: Map the Journey

Now compare the before and after:

- What do they feel *before* they engage with your brand?
- What do you want them to feel *after?*

Let's say your dream client is overwhelmed, skeptical, and unsure.

After working with you, you want them to feel confident, clear, and empowered.

Boom. That's part of your brand word map right there.

Phase Four: Describe Without Diluting

Make a list of 20 to 30 adjectives or short descriptors that *might* fit. Don't judge or edit yet.

Once you have your list, review each one and ask:

- *Is it emotionally specific?*
- *Does it actually apply to my brand today (not just my vision)?*
- *Can I show up in this word—visually, verbally, energetically—across platforms?*

Cut anything generic (like "cool," "fun," "unique"). Replace them with something sharper: "irreverent," "vibrant," "one-of-a-kind," "boundary-pushing," etc.

Aim to narrow your list to three to five. Then pressure-test them.

Phase Five: Pressure-Test in Context

Put your final brand words to work:

- Can you write a caption that reflects this word?
- Does your headshot, logo, or website design match this word's energy?
- Would your clients or customers describe you this way?

And the big one: Would you want this word to be used when you're introduced on a podcast, quoted in a feature, or spoken about in a room you haven't entered yet?

If yes, keep it. If not, it's out.

Real Brand Word Examples in the Wild

Still wondering how powerful brand words really are? Let's look at how a few iconic brands use them, not just to describe their identity but to *build entire empires* around how they make people feel.

Drybar

Drybar isn't just selling blowouts, they're selling transformation. And they've built a wildly successful beauty brand around just a few carefully chosen words:

- Confident
- Fun
- Consistent
- Feminine

From their bright yellow branding and cheeky cocktail-themed product names to the ultra-reliable experience you get at every location, Drybar has created a feeling that women can count on. They don't just offer hair services. They offer confidence-on-demand in an environment that feels playful, polished, and a little bit VIP.

Every touchpoint—from the smell of the shampoo to the upbeat playlists—is rooted in their brand words.

Coca-Cola

The Coca-Cola brand has lasted over a century not because it has the best soda, but because it owns a set of deeply emotional brand words:

- Happiness
- Togetherness
- Classic
- Refreshing

Whether it's a holiday ad, a polar bear animation, or a Coke bottle with your name on it, everything about their brand reinforces the feeling of joy and connection. Coca-Cola is less about quenching thirst and more about nostalgia, comfort, and shared experience. That's no accident; it's masterful use of brand language.

Lululemon

Lululemon isn't just yoga pants. It's identity. It's aspiration. It's a lifestyle. Their brand words help them command a premium price tag, and fierce loyalty:

- Empowered
- Performance
- Intentional
- Elevated

Their copy, campaigns, store layouts, and even employee training all reinforce these ideas. They don't just talk about leggings—they talk about mindset. Goals. Strength. Inner power. If you've ever walked out of a Lululemon feeling like you suddenly had better posture or higher standards, you've felt the effect of brand words in action.

Spanx

Spanx didn't become a billion-dollar brand by selling shapewear. It became a cultural phenomenon by solving a problem women didn't know they were allowed to talk about. And then building a brand voice that said, "I get it. And I've got you."

Their brand words?

- Empowering
- Clever
- Real
- Unapologetic

Everything about Spanx, down to the packaging copy, feels like a best friend who also happens to be a badass CEO. Founder Sara Blakely made "shapewear" not just acceptable, but aspirational, by infusing humor, honesty, and high standards into every brand touchpoint.

You see it in the cheeky product names. The confident tone of voice. The way Spanx shows up in the media, on shelves, and in the lives of women who want to feel powerful *and* comfortable.

The result? A brand that isn't just worn. It's trusted.

When done right, brand words aren't just descriptors. They become the filter for *every single choice*—design, messaging, packaging, partnerships, storytelling, and service.

That's the secret. Brand words aren't fluff. They're focus.

What If You Get It "Wrong"?

Spoiler alert: you won't.

You're allowed to evolve. As you grow, your brand words may shift slightly, but their essence will remain. That's the beauty of building a brand on values, voice, and vibe. Not trends.

Try them on. Speak them out loud. See how they feel in an email, in a podcast pitch, or on your About page.

Your words will meet you where you are, and carry you where you're going.

Pitchworthy Power Move

Your brand words are your anchor and amplifier.

Use them to guide how you show up *and* how you scale. Every campaign, pitch, caption, and partnership should pass the test: *Does this sound like us?*

PR Myth You Can Ditch

"Professional means polished—and polished means generic."

False.

Polished *without personality* is forgettable. Professional *with precision* is iconic. Your brand words make you unforgettable.

Pitchworthy Prompt

If a dream client described your brand to their best friend, what three words would you *want* them to use?

Write them down. Now go earn them.

CHAPTER 5

Kickass Key Messages

In a world of scroll-stopping visuals, it's tempting to think a pretty feed or aesthetic brand is enough.

But here's the truth:

It's not the look that sells. It's the language.

Attention goes to the message that's sharp, simple, and impossible to forget.

If you want to stand out, be remembered, and drive visibility that actually converts, you need more than design. You need definition.

And it starts with key messages.

The Most Important Words in Your Business

Let me be blunt: Key messages aren't just a branding exercise. They're *nonnegotiable*.

They're how your brand introduces itself.

They're what your customers remember.

They're what the media repeats.

And they're what people share when you're not in the room.

In PR, they're everything.

What Exactly *Are* Key Messages?

Key messages are the sharpest, clearest, most memorable statements that explain who you are, what you do, and why it matters.

They're not elevator pitches.

They're not one-liners or taglines.

They're strategic soundbites that can be pulled for interviews, used in media bios, dropped into a press release, or delivered on stage in seven seconds flat.

They are:

- Concise
- Confident
- Repeatable
- Rooted in your brand values
- Aligned with your audience's desires

Think of them as your communication anchors. The stronger they are, the less explaining you'll have to do, and the faster your message lands.

Why They Matter So Damn Much

Let's be honest: The internet is loud. And attention spans are short.

If someone clicks to your website, sees your social post, or hears your name mentioned, you've got about five seconds to make an impression.

Your key messages do the heavy lifting.

They don't just describe your business, they position it. They help people *get it*, and more importantly, *remember it*.

Strong key messages also:

- Guide your brand voice across platforms
- Help team members and collaborators stay consistent
- Serve as the backbone for media pitches, interviews, bios, and copy
- Create alignment in how your audience sees and speaks about you

And when you're ready for press? They're the first thing a journalist or podcast host will quote.

The Formula for Crafting Kickass Key Messages

Don't overcomplicate it.

You don't need poetry. You need clarity. You're aiming for three to four simple, sharp, emotionally compelling statements.

Follow this step-by-step approach:

1. Start with Why

   Why are you doing what you do?

   Why does it matter to your audience?

   Why should anyone care now?

   If you can answer those questions in one sentence each, you're halfway there.

2. Make It Believable

   Avoid hype. Be specific. Use proof or context when you can.

   Instead of: "We're the best in the business."

   Try: "We've helped over 5,000 founders land media coverage that actually grows their business."

   That's clear, credible, and repeatable.

3. Keep It Short

   Aim for one sentence per message. Two, max.

   Your audience should be able to understand and repeat your messages without taking notes. If they can't paraphrase what you said to a colleague? It's too complicated.

4. Know Your Audience

   What does your audience actually want from you?

   Key messages should speak directly to their needs, values, and desires.

What are they afraid of? What do they crave? What are they Googling at 3:00 a.m.?

Speak to that.

5. Reflect Your Brand Words

This is where your brand words come back in.

If your brand words are "empowering," "bold," and "grounded," your key messages should *sound* that way. They're not meant to be copy-pasted from a business plan. They should feel alive, emotional, and like *you*.

A Real-World Example: Spanx

Let's apply this in the wild.

For a brand like Spanx, key messages might sound like:

- *Spanx creates shapewear, apparel, and activewear designed by women, for women.*
- *We believe confidence begins underneath, and every body deserves to feel amazing.*
- *Our mission is to make getting dressed the easiest, most empowering part of your day.*
- *Founded by a woman with $5,000 and a big idea, Spanx has redefined comfort, style, and success.*

Notice how every sentence:

- Uses plain, emotional language
- Aligns with their brand words (empowering, clever, real, unapologetic)
- Could be dropped into a podcast, press piece, or investor pitch with zero editing

That's the level of polish we're going for.

A Second Real-World Example: Glossier

Let's look at another brand that nailed their messaging from day one: *Glossier*.

Glossier built a multimillion-dollar beauty empire with a product line that, at first glance, looked like everyone else's: moisturizer, lip balm, mascara. So how did they stand out? By writing key messages that felt *radically personal* in an industry that had historically been aspirational, airbrushed, and out of touch.

Here's what Glossier's early key messages might have looked like:

- *Glossier is beauty inspired by real life.*
- *We believe you're already beautiful, and your makeup should reflect that.*
- *Our products are designed to live with you, not on top of you.*
- *We make skincare and makeup that starts with you, not a professional artist.*

Every word reinforced their brand words: approachable, minimal, modern, and real. Their messaging didn't compete with legacy beauty brands, it rewrote the rules entirely. And that disruption came straight from a few sentences that told a very different kind of story.

Make Your Messages Work Harder

Once you've written your key messages, put them to work:

- On your website's About page
- In your social bios
- At the top of your press kit
- Inside every media pitch
- As pull quotes in your email newsletters
- In how you introduce yourself on stage, in interviews, or in your email signature

They're not meant to live in a document and collect digital dust. They're meant to *circulate*.

Keep Them Fresh

Your business evolves. Your audience evolves.

So should your key messages.

Schedule a check-in every six months, or after a major launch, pivot, or rebrand, to review:

- Are these still true?
- Do they still reflect who we are and where we're going?
- Are they helping or holding us back?

Great brands evolve. So do great brand messages.

Common Mistakes to Avoid

Now let's talk about what *not* to do.

Weak key messages often:

- Sound like a mission statement written by committee
- Use vague buzzwords like "innovative" or "high quality" with no context
- Include too many ideas at once
- Don't differentiate from competitors
- Can't be spoken out loud with confidence

Here's what that looks like in the wild:

"Our brand believes in solutions that prioritize customer success through forward-thinking innovation and high-quality experiences."

. . . *What?*

That could be a bank. A tech startup. A toothpaste company. It says *nothing* and tries to say *everything*.

Great key messages are clear, emotionally resonant, and specific enough to only describe *you*.

From Meh to Magnetic: A Key Message Makeover

Let's take a fictional example and workshop it together:

Let's say the business is a high-end home organizing company.

GOOD: "We help clients get organized so they can enjoy their homes more."

Nice . . . but generic. Could be anyone.

BETTER: "We design custom home organizing solutions that help clients reduce clutter and reclaim calm."

Now we're getting more specific—problem and benefit. Still a little safe.

BEST: "We believe peace of mind starts in your pantry. Our luxury organizing services transform chaos into calm and make staying organized effortless."

That's a whole *vibe*. It speaks to the target client, reflects clear brand words (luxury, calm, intentional), and could go straight into a pitch, press quote, or podcast intro.

That's the goal.

Workshop Your Key Messages

Let's make this personal. Grab a pen or open your Notes app and answer these questions:

- If someone googled you today, what's the one sentence you *wish* they'd find at the top of the search results?
- What problem do you solve—and what's the bigger story or belief behind it?
- If your dream client described your business in one sentence, what would you want them to say?
- What emotions should your key messages evoke? Confidence? Relief? Excitement? Clarity?
- How do you want to be introduced at your next panel, podcast, or press interview?

Answer these honestly, and you'll start to see the bones of your key messages take shape. Refine, test, and tighten until they feel like *truth on the page.*

Pitchworthy Power Move

Key messages aren't filler copy. They're your proof of positioning.

If you can't say what you do in a way that excites people to talk about you, you're not done yet.

PR Myth You Can Ditch

"Your work speaks for itself."

No, it doesn't. You do.

Even the best work needs words that frame it, sell it, and help others talk about it when you're not in the room.

Pitchworthy Prompt

Pull up your current About page or bio. Would a stranger reading it immediately understand who you are, what you offer, and what makes you different?

If not—start rewriting from your key messages.

CHAPTER 6

Elevating Your Elevator Speech

Let's talk about the first time I had to deliver an elevator speech on my own. No crutch, no wing woman, no do-over.

It was one of those stuffy, early-evening networking events where everyone clutches a drink like a life raft and pretends they love *When you've only got seconds, every word counts.* small talk. I stood there, palms sweating, heart pounding, wishing I could melt into the wallpaper.

I knew I had something to say, I just didn't know how to say it. Not in a way that felt clear. Or confident. Or anything close to magnetic.

That day was a disaster.

It was also the catalyst for a skill that's since unlocked rooms, clients, and interviews I only dreamed of.

Because when you can say who you are and what you do with clarity, conviction, and a little charisma? People listen. Doors open. Media leans in.

And if you're reading this, you're ready to elevate your own elevator speech. Let's do it.

Why Elevator Speeches Matter

Let's get something straight: Your elevator speech isn't just a party trick or PR prep. It's your story in scalpel-sharp form.

If you had less than 30 seconds to tell someone:

- Who you are
- What you do
- And how you can help them

. . . what would you say?

Could you do it in two sentences or less?

Because in today's world, that's the window you've got. The average human attention span? Shorter than a goldfish's. Just six seconds.

When someone asks, "What do you do?" you'd better have an answer that makes them stop scrolling, lean in, and think: *I need more of that.*

Your elevator speech should sell curiosity. Authority. A little sparkle.

Because when you nail it? It opens doors faster than any business card.

What Is an Elevator Speech, Really?

By definition, an elevator speech is a short summary of who you are and what you do, designed to leave an impression in 30 seconds or less.

But let's be real: Most elevator speeches sound like bad dating profiles: too vague, too long, or totally forgettable.

"I'm a business coach who helps people reach their goals."

Cool. So is every other business coach on LinkedIn.

A Pitchworthy elevator speech, on the other hand, is magnetic. It's tight, memorable, and makes people want to learn more.

Think of it like a trailer for your brand: short, compelling, and strategically designed to spark interest.

Anatomy of a Powerful Speech

Your elevator speech should include:

- Who you are
- Who you help
- What you help them achieve

- Why it matters
- A hook or point of intrigue

You don't need to say all of that word for word. But the best elevator speeches hit each of these implicitly, and with style.

Now, remember your brand words and key messages? This is where they really shine.

When your pitch includes the same emotional language you want your brand to be known for, it reinforces every single other piece of your visibility strategy—from bios to headlines to media intros.

Before → After → Pitchworthy

Let's look at a fictional brand and elevate their elevator speech using a good > better > best approach.

Brand Example: Indie skincare founder

Audience: Women 35+ with sensitive skin

Good: "I make skincare products that are clean and natural."

Better: "My brand helps women with sensitive skin feel confident using clean, simple products."

Pitchworthy: "I help women over 35 calm sensitive skin, without 12-step routines or toxic ingredients. Because skincare shouldn't stress you out."

Notice the shift? The last version speaks directly to a specific audience, solves a problem, uses emotionally resonant language, and positions the brand as a solution—not just a product.

Real Brand Example: Glossier

Let's take a real-world look at Glossier, the beauty brand that built a cult following by flipping the beauty industry script.

Here's how Glossier might introduce itself in an elevator speech:

"Glossier is a beauty brand inspired by real people. We believe skin should look like skin, and makeup should enhance, not hide. Our products are designed to make you feel good in your own skin."

What makes it work?

- Conversational tone
- Values-forward ("inspired by real people")
- Emphasis on transformation and ease
- Brand words like "natural," "effortless," and "confident" built right in

It's not about listing products. It's about identity, emotion, and belief. And that's what makes it Pitchworthy.

Industry-Specific Examples

Need help making this real? Let's look at how a few different industries might pitch themselves.

Interior Designer

"I design bold, functional homes for high-achieving women who want to love where they live and show it off with pride."

Tech Startup Founder

"I'm building an AI platform that helps freelancers run their business without burnout, by automating the stuff they hate."

Business Coach

"I help entrepreneurs stop second-guessing and start scaling, using a strategy that works *with* their brain, not against it."

Realtor

"I help first-time homebuyers in Austin find homes they love, without overpaying or getting ghosted by agents."

Nonprofit Founder

"We create job opportunities for refugee women through hand-made textiles, so every piece you buy helps change a life."

The goal? Position yourself as the solution your audience didn't know they needed yet can't forget.

Common Elevator Pitch Mistakes

Here's what doesn't work, and why.

Too vague: "I'm in branding."

What does that even mean? For who? Why should I care?

Too long: "Well, I actually got into coaching after a pivot from real estate, and now I help clients with mindset, but also business, and . . ."

Yawn. You've already lost them.

Too self-focused: "I'm a digital nomad building my brand." Cool story, bro, but what's in it for your audience?

Your pitch isn't a memoir. It's a value statement. Lead with what they get, not what you do.

Crafting Yours: Six Steps

Here's how to get yours from "meh" to "magnetic":

1. Brain Dump

   Write 10 ways to describe what you do. Don't filter, just let it out.

2. Identify Your Goal

   Is this for attracting clients? Getting media coverage? Opening partnerships?

3. Develop Action Statements

   Write 10 power statements (like "I help . . .," "I create . . .," "I solve . . .").

4. Say It Out Loud

   Record yourself saying a few versions. Which one feels clear and confident?

5. Get Feedback

   Test it on trusted friends or industry peers. Watch where they nod, or glaze over.

6. Tighten It

   Edit down to 30 seconds or about 100 words. Make every word work.

Then? Practice it. Obsessively. Until you can say it in your sleep, or at least with a second glass of wine.

Worksheet: Craft Your Pitchworthy Intro

Use this framework to build your elevator speech step-by-step. You don't have to use every line verbatim—but each one will help you layer in clarity and intrigue.

1. Who are you? "I'm a _____ who helps _____."

   Example: "I'm a financial educator who helps women ditch shame and take control of their money."

2. What's the transformation? "I help them go from _____ to _____."

   Example: "from confused and anxious to confident and in control."

3. What makes your approach different? "My secret sauce is _____."

   Example: "a mix of behavioral science and unapologetic honesty."

4. Why should they care? "This matters because _____."

   Example: "everyone deserves financial security—no matter their past."

5. Your one-liner version: "I help creative founders turn media attention into long-term credibility, without selling out or burning out."

Practice out loud. Tweak until it sounds like you. Say it to a stranger. A dream client. A barista. Until it rolls off your tongue like gospel. That's how you know it's Pitchworthy.

The One-Liner Test

Once you've got your full elevator speech nailed, challenge yourself to distill it into one unforgettable line for email intros, bios, or social captions.

Example: "I help founders become the talk of the town, through visibility strategies that actually convert."

If your one-liner makes someone say, "Tell me more," you've nailed it.

Publicity Practice

Now it's your turn. Use these prompts to shape, refine, and elevate your elevator pitch:

- *What transformation do I create for my audience?*
- *What belief does my brand embody?*
- *Which words do I want people to associate with my work?*
- *What's my 30-second speech?*
- *What's my one-liner version?*

Say it out loud. Say it again. Then say it at every opportunity. Because in this industry, it's not just what you do, it's how powerfully you can say it.

Pitchworthy Power Move

Turn your elevator speech into a signature email sign-off. Use a single sentence in your email footer or pitches that sums up your brilliance.

"Helping entrepreneurs go from best-kept secret to go-to source, one media hit at a time."

Better yet, once you've perfected your one-liner, test it everywhere: Instagram bio, Zoom intro, email signature. The more you say it, the more you believe it. And so will they.

PR Myth You Can Ditch

"If you build it, they'll come."

Nope. They won't. Not unless you know how to introduce yourself in a way that makes them care.

Start with a strong pitch, and the visibility will follow.

Pitchworthy Prompt

What's the boldest, clearest way you can describe what you do in one sentence?

Bonus: Would your dream client or a podcast host want to know more?

CHAPTER 7

Making Your Media List

You've got an elevator speech so good it makes your competitors sweat. The angle is sharp. The story's airtight. You're ready to hit send . . .

Except . . . you're not quite sure who to send it to.

The magic is in pitching the right person, not everyone.

Welcome to the all-too-common limbo between publicity potential and media coverage.

What stands between you and press? The right people. Which means the right list.

This chapter is your hands-on guide to building a Pitchworthy media list—the kind that gets your story into inboxes (and then into headlines).

Because the truth is: Even the most brilliant pitch will flop if it's sent to the wrong person.

Let's fix that.

What Is a Media List (and Why Do You Need One)?

Think of your media list as your backstage pass to visibility. It's a curated, strategic contact sheet of the journalists, editors, freelancers, producers, podcasters, newsletter creators, bloggers—and yes, influencers—who actually care about your story and have the platform to amplify it.

It's less "spray and pray," more "sniper-level precision."

A great media list is:

- Specific
- Strategic
- Always evolving
- And full of people who have covered similar brands, topics, or trends before

Gone are the days when sending your pitch to *info@publication.com* was enough. That's a fast track to being ghosted by the press.

Who Belongs on Your List

Spoiler alert: Not everyone.

One of the biggest rookie mistakes? Trying to pitch to *every* outlet, hoping something sticks. Instead, you want to build a list of aligned, high-fit contacts who are most likely to say yes.

Start with your audience.

Ask:

- Where do they spend time?
- What do they read, watch, scroll, or subscribe to?
- Who do they trust as a voice in your space?

If your ideal client is a stylish 40-something mom juggling work, wellness, and design inspiration, your targets might include *Real Simple*, *The Cut*, *HGTV Magazine*, or *The Skimm*.

If you're in B2B tech? Your dream outlets might include *Fast Company*, *TechCrunch*, or an industry trade pub that makes most people yawn, but makes your buyer sit up straighter.

Think multi-platform.

Your media list might include:

- Magazine editors
- TV producers
- Morning show bookers
- Newspaper reporters

- Substack authors
- Freelancers who write for five outlets (these are *gold*)
- Podcast hosts
- LinkedIn thought leaders
- TikTok creators who recap business news

Media isn't just print or pixel anymore, it's omnichannel. And your media list should reflect that.

How to Build Your List from Scratch

Here's your step-by-step blueprint:

1. Google Like a Publicist

   Search for recent articles about your niche or angle. Take note of:

   - Byline names
   - Outlet names
   - Article angles
   - Contact info in the author bios

   Example: Searching "colorful interior design small space" might lead you to a Domino editor who *loves* bold before-and-afters.

2. Mine Your Competition

   Where have your peers or competitors been featured? Their press pages equals your prospecting goldmine.

3. Check Social Media

   Journalists often post their latest work or what they're currently looking for (especially on X/Twitter and Threads). Follow them. Engage. Then pitch.

4. Hit the Masthead

Old-school? Yes. Still works? Absolutely. Flip to the front of any magazine. You'll find editors by title, section, and sometimes even email format.

5. Use Smart Tools (If You Can)

If budget allows, invest in databases like Muck Rack, Prowly, or Qwoted. But honestly? You can build a killer list with Google, LinkedIn, and your brain.

How to Organize It Like a Pro

Use a spreadsheet. No fancy CRM needed.
Create columns for:

- Outlet name
- Contact name
- Title
- Email
- Notes (include past stories they've written or angles they love)
- Pitch date and follow-up date

Color-code by tier if you want:

- Tier 1 = Dream coverage (high visibility, aligned audience)
- Tier 2 = Targeted but smaller reach
- Tier 3 = Local media or niche blogs

Set yourself up to *track*, *follow up*, and *refine* over time. You're not building a one-time list. You're building a press pipeline.

Common Mistakes to Avoid

1. Using outdated info. Editors move constantly. Always double-check contacts before pitching.

2. Mass-blasting generic pitches. If your email starts with "Hi there," it's headed for the trash. Use names. Reference work. Be human.

3. Pitching the wrong section. Don't send your new beauty product to the tech editor. Even if she's nice, it's not her job to pass it along.

4. Only targeting national outlets. Local press, podcasts, and newsletters are often easier wins, and build momentum for bigger hits.

A Real-Life Example

Let's say you're a wellness entrepreneur launching a line of adaptogenic teas.

Here's what your Tier 1 media list *might* include:

- Well+Good (health and wellness resource)
- *Bon Appétit* (foodie audience)
- *The Cut* (trendy, urban female readership)
- Morning show producers from *Good Morning America* and the *TODAY* Show
- Freelancer writing for both *Vogue* and *Goop* on holistic health

You'd research who covers tea, adaptogens, morning routines, and functional beverages. Read their recent work. Connect online. Then pitch.

That's media list magic.

How to Keep It Fresh

Set a quarterly date to audit your list:

- Are your contacts still there?
- Have they switched beats?
- Is there a new podcast or Substack that's hot with your audience?

Keep your eyes peeled. Media is a revolving door. Editors turn into freelancers. Interns turn into gatekeepers. Stay on top of the game, and your list will stay hot.

Publicity Practice

Now it's your turn to get your hands dirty, in the most glamorous, strategic way possible.

- Start your spreadsheet.
- Choose three dream outlets.
- Google who's writing what in your space.
- Add 10 contacts to start. Yes, just 10.
- Commit to building it weekly.

Remember, a small but mighty media list is more powerful than a bloated, outdated one. Quality over quantity. Always.

Pitchworthy Power Move

Google this phrase today: "site: [outlet.com] + your topic."

Example: site: wellandgood.com adaptogens

You'll find who's writing about your space, what angle they used, and who to add to your list.

That's how publicists pull contacts *without* a paid database.

PR Myth You Can Ditch

"If you build a good pitch, the press will find you."

Nope. Reporters are swamped, understaffed, and overwhelmed. It's *your* job to get your story in front of the right person and make their job easier. That starts with a killer list.

Pitchworthy Prompt

Write down five places you dream of being featured. Then answer:

- Who is the actual *person* who would write the piece?
- What kinds of stories do they cover?
- What makes your story a fit?

This is how you stop blindly pitching and start building relationships that lead to results.

CHAPTER 8

Creating Content Calendars

Let's just say it: I'm obsessed with this chapter.

Call it a personal favorite, call it a professional flex—this is where everything starts to click.

There is nothing more thrilling to me than helping a founder see the year ahead laid out in strategic, Pitchworthy opportunities. It's where

Consistency beats chaos when it comes to visibility.

ideas stop collecting dust and start becoming headlines.

Because, friend, your brand is full of stories. Real ones. And PR-worthy ones. But if you don't map them out? You're setting yourself up for stress, missed moments, and a PR plan that lives in your head instead of in the world.

Let's fix that. Let's build your content calendar.

What Is a Content Calendar?

Think of it as your publicity GPS.

A content calendar (a.k.a. promo calendar, editorial calendar, or pitch calendar) is a 12-month map of what you plan to share with the public, and when. It lays out:

- What you're talking about
- Why it matters now
- Where it fits into your PR goals

A proper content calendar aligns your launches, sales, and stories with seasonal trends, national moments, and industry timelines.

It helps you:

- Stay consistent
- Anticipate opportunities
- Keep your messaging sharp
- Avoid that "What the heck should I post?" panic

And if you're thinking, *KJ, I'm already drowning in launches, logistics, and lead magnets. Why add one more thing?* The short answer? Because this is the thing that keeps everything else in motion.

Without a content calendar, your promotions get sporadic. Your brand voice becomes inconsistent. And your PR strategy turns into a game of chance.

We're not here for that. We're here for momentum.

Why You Need a Content Calendar

Let's get into the strategy of it.

A content calendar does three powerful things:

1. It keeps you consistent. PR isn't a one-and-done game. It's a visibility habit. That means showing up over time, with relevant messages, tailored to your audience. A calendar makes it sustainable.
2. It brings clarity to chaos. Have too many ideas and don't know where to start? A content calendar gives them a home. Feel like you have nothing to say? Your calendar shows you exactly what's next.
3. It becomes your brand archive. Ever forgotten what you promoted last spring? What pitch landed a client two years ago? Your calendar becomes your PR memory bank, and lets you double down on what's worked.

It also lets you audit your mix: Are you educating? Entertaining? Selling? Too much take, not enough give? This is where my 3GT Rule comes in.

The 3GT Rule

Three gives to every take.

For every one promotional post (a sale, a pitch, a press mention), share three educational, engaging, or entertaining pieces of content.

Why? Because people don't want to be sold to 24/7. They want to connect with your ideas, your values, and your vibe.

This balance builds trust. And trust builds influence.

The Step-by-Step Content Calendar Process

Here's how I build 12-month calendars for top brands. You can use it too, whether you're running a lifestyle brand, an interior design firm, or a startup about to launch.

1. Choose Your Format

    Analog or digital? Choose a system that you'll actually use:

    - A Google Sheet
    - Airtable
    - A massive desk calendar (my personal favorite)

    Your call. Just commit to one.

2. Mark the Big Stuff

    Add these to your calendar:

    - Product launches
    - Sales and promos
    - Speaking gigs
    - Brand milestones
    - Campaigns

    These are your anchors.

3. Add Holidays and Seasonal Moments

Now layer in:

- National holidays (think Valentine's Day, Mother's Day, Thanksgiving)
- Marketing holidays (think Small Business Saturday, International Women's Day, National Coffee Day)
- Seasonal content (think summer travel, back-to-school, fall nesting)

Not every holiday matters. Choose what's relevant to your brand and audience.

Example: If you're a luxury dress brand? Easter, wedding season, and holiday party dressing matter. If you're a parenting expert? Back-to-school, summer travel, and holiday hacks are gold.

4. Add Industry Relevance

What's trending in your space this month, season, or quarter? Include:

- Editorial calendars from magazines
- Seasonal buyer behavior
- Conference or trade show schedules
- Relevant news cycles or cultural trends

This is how you stay timely *and* strategic.

5. Brainstorm Weekly or Monthly Themes

Go month by month and ask:

- *What do I want to be known for this month?*
- *What stories, ideas, or products deserve a spotlight?*
- *What does my audience need right now?*

If you're stuck, start with these prompts:

- *What questions do I always get?*
- *What myths do I want to bust?*
- *What do I wish people knew?*
- *What would I shout from a stage if I had five minutes?*

Good Calendars Lead to Great Pitches

You don't create a content calendar to feel busy. You create one so you always know where your pitch fits into the bigger picture.

A well-built calendar gives you:

- A reason to pitch
- A story to tell
- The lead time to pull it off

If you're launching a capsule collection in May? You start pitching spring style in February. If you want to be featured in a December gift guide? You start planning in July.

That's why this work matters. It puts *you* in the driver's seat.

Keep It Fresh

Remember: This isn't set-it-and-forget-it. Great content calendars are flexible. They evolve. They get better the more you use them.

Give yourself permission to:

- Adjust as news breaks
- Shift themes if something flops
- Layer in new ideas as you grow

The goal is not perfection. The goal is preparation.

Pitchworthy Power Move

Pull out your calendar and mark your next 90 days. Add three promotional moments (a launch, event, or campaign) and back into them by three weeks. That's your new pitching runway. Treat it like your personal Fashion Week calendar.

PR Myth You Can Ditch

"You have to post every day to stay relevant."

REALITY: You have to show up *consistently* with value. That might mean two times a week with intention beats seven posts of chaos.

Pitchworthy Prompt

What's one seasonal event or holiday that your brand *should* own? Brainstorm three storylines you could pitch around it.

CHAPTER 9

Pitching Perfection

You've done the brand work. You've refined your message. You've mapped your content and media lists. Now comes the part everyone either obsesses over . . . or avoids like the plague:

Craft the kind of pitch editors actually want to open.

The Pitch

Let me be clear: If your pitch isn't landing, it's not because the media doesn't like you.

It's because your story either isn't clear enough, or it's not compelling enough for the inbox it landed in.

Good news? We're about to fix that.

Whether you're chasing a feature in *Forbes* or you want your product on the morning news, everything starts with the pitch. A smart one. A specific one. A Pitchworthy one.

So let's get yours in shape.

What Is a Media Pitch, Really?

At its core, a media pitch is a personalized story idea you send to a journalist, editor, or producer, offering them something worth sharing with their audience. Think of it as an editorial introduction:

"Hey [Insert Dream Outlet], here's a story your readers will love, and here's why I'm the one to tell it."

Unlike a press release (which is more formal, polished, and widely distributed), your pitch is a relationship-building tool. It's direct. Intentional. And ideally, the start of a long and mutually beneficial conversation.

The best pitches read like a confident whisper in a crowded room: "I know what you need, and I've got the story to match."

Why It Matters (More Than You Think)

A pitch isn't just about publicity. It's about positioning.
Done right, a pitch does more than score media coverage. It:

- Shapes how your audience sees you
- Builds trust and credibility through third-party validation
- Shows your expertise in real-world, relatable context
- Drives traffic, awareness, and opportunities without the cost of an ad

This is how unknowns become go-to voices. This is how brands scale fast. This is how you go from "aspiring" to "quoted in *Vogue*."

And here's the kicker: Most people don't pitch at all. Or they pitch once, get ghosted, and give up.

Which is your chance to stand out with strategy and consistency.

The Five Pitch Angles That Actually Work

Let's break down the five Pitchworthy angles every founder, expert, or creative should keep on speed dial. These aren't theories, they're formats I've used to place clients in everything from the *TODAY* Show to *Fast Company*.

1. Evergreen Pitches

    These are timeless. Always relevant. They're not tied to trends or seasons, and they perform year-round.

Examples:

- "5 Things Designers Wish You Knew Before Renovating Your Kitchen"
- "How to Stop Making This Expensive Mistake in Your Business Finances"
- "What to Do When Your Brand Stops Growing"

Pro Tip: How-tos and lists work best here.

2. Seasonal Pitches

Think spring cleaning. Back-to-school. Holiday gift guides. These align with real-world timing, cultural rhythms, and consumer behaviors.

Examples:

- "The Summer Wardrobe Swap That's Actually Worth It"
- "Top 10 Mother's Day Gifts That Aren't Just Candles"
- "Fall Reset Rituals Every Entrepreneur Should Steal"

Pitch these one to three months in advance. Editors plan ahead.

3. Marketing Holidays

From National Pet Day to World Mental Health Day, marketing holidays give you built-in relevance, if you choose the right one.

Examples:

- "Why This Founder Built Her Wellness Brand on International Self-Care Day"
- "This Latina Business Owner Is Redefining Leadership During Hispanic Heritage Month"

Bonus: These angles do great on morning shows and lifestyle blogs.

4. Newsjacking

This is your chance to jump on a trending topic and inject your POV or expertise. Done right, it's powerful. Done wrong, it's cringe.

Examples:

- "What Beyoncé's Tour Merch Teaches Us About Brand Loyalty"
- "As AI Reshapes Design, Here's What Human Creativity Still Does Better"

Stay swift and classy. You're not here to ride waves, you're here to shape the conversation.

5. Promotional Pitches

These are product drops, launches, campaigns. Be sparing here. Media doesn't owe you coverage because you're launching something new.

But if it's timely, relevant, and valuable to their audience? You've got a shot.

Examples:

- "Just Dropped: The First-Ever Inclusive Planner for Neurodiverse Professionals"
- "Dallas-Based Designer Launches Luxury Line That's Reclaiming Southern Maximalism"

The Dos and Don'ts of Pitching

DO:

- Personalize every pitch by referencing their recent work.
- Lead with a compelling subject line.
- Include links, visuals, and your contact info.

- Keep it tight: under 250 words.
- Follow up politely after three to five business days.

DON'T:

- Bury your angle. Make it obvious, fast.
- Attach big files. Use links.
- Mass email without blind copy. (Rookie mistake.)
- Over-apologize or oversell. Respect the inbox.

Common Pitch Pitfalls to Avoid

You're smart. You're ready. But I've seen even the best founders fall into these traps:

- Being too vague: "We're passionate about helping people live better lives." Okay, but how?
- Making it all about you: The story needs to serve *their* audience.
- Pitching at the wrong time: You can't pitch a holiday gift guide on December 15.
- Forgetting the ask: Tell them what you want—an interview, a feature, a product roundup mention?

Pitching is not the place to play coy. Be bold and be blunt.

The Anatomy of a Pitchworthy Pitch

By now, you know what makes a pitch sing: It's relevant. It's timely. It's written for a specific human, not "Dear Editor." It shows, not sells. It connects your story to the bigger picture.

But even with all that knowledge, sometimes you need to see it in action to really *feel* it.

So let's break down a real-deal, ready-to-send pitch—one you can model your own after.

Scenario:

Let's say you're the founder of a luxury candle company that just released a new scent inspired by the quiet power of women who get sh*t done. You're pitching it to the style editor at a national lifestyle outlet known for trend pieces and gift guides.

Subject line:

This luxury candle is what "quiet luxury" smells like

Email pitch:

Hello Jordan,

I wanted to share something I thought might catch your eye, especially with so many of your readers leaning into slow, intentional living this fall.

I'm the founder of Eli & Mae, a female-founded candle studio inspired by the stillness (and strength) of women who carry the weight of the world—and make it look good.

Our newest scent, Inheritance, blends fig leaf, amber, and a trace of black pepper. It's a subtle nod to the idea of "quiet luxury," but for the home.

I think it could be a perfect fit for an upcoming trend roundup, fall gifting feature, or even a piece on rituals or cozy design.

I've linked our lookbook, hi-res images, and the full scent story below, but am happy to send samples if you'd like to test it out.

Many thanks,

KJ Blattenbauer

Founder, Eli & Mae
[Phone]
[Website or press page link]
[Dropbox/Google Drive folder with media assets]

Why This Works:

Personalized: You're speaking *to* the editor and referencing their editorial POV, not blasting them with a generic intro.

- Timely: It ties into current trends ("quiet luxury," fall rituals).
- Visual: It paints a picture but leaves room for the editor's creativity.
- Service-minded: It offers assets, samples, and story fit suggestions, making their job easier.

Final Thought

Good pitches don't brag. They build bridges.
They say: "Here's something your readers will love."
Not: "Here's something I really want you to cover."
That shift? That's what makes it Pitchworthy.

Where the Magic Happens

Let's say you've got your pitch written. What next?
Start with your media list. Pull 10 to 15 dream outlets and contacts. Research their work. Draft personalized pitches for each. Keep a tracker. Follow up. Repeat.
This isn't spray-and-pray PR. This is precision. Persistence. Positioning.
This is how you stop hoping to be discovered and start controlling your narrative.

Following Up Like a Pro (Without Being Annoying)

So you've crafted a strong pitch. Hit send. And now . . . silence.
This is where most people panic, second-guess, or ghost their own strategy. Don't be most people.

Following Up Is Not Pestering—It's Part of the Process

The media is swamped. They get hundreds of emails a day, and yours probably landed between a breaking news alert and a press release about gluten-free dog shampoo.

So here's how to follow up without feeling like a stage-five clinger:

When to Follow Up

Wait three to five business days after sending your pitch before following up. Not counting weekends. Not counting holidays. Real business days. Respect the rhythm of their world.

If it's a seasonal or time-sensitive pitch (say, tied to an upcoming event or launch), lead with that urgency in your follow-up.

How to Follow Up

Keep it short. Friendly. Direct.

Here's a quick template:

Subject line: Following up: Story idea on [insert angle]

Hello [First Name],

I wanted to follow up on the pitch I sent earlier this week about [remind them of the hook].

Let me know if you're working on anything this could be a fit for, or if there's someone else on your team I should reach out to.

Happy to resend the details or share supporting visuals if helpful.

Thanks again for your time!

[Your Name]

This tone says: "I'm helpful and proactive, not desperate for attention."

What to Do If You Still Hear Nothing

Don't spiral. Do this instead:

- Give it another five to seven business days before trying a second follow-up (max of three touches total).
- If still no response? Move on. Pitch a different angle. Or circle back a few weeks later with something new.

And if the story is time-sensitive, follow your second email with a polite phone call or DM (if they're open to that). One touchpoint per channel, max.

Persistence is professional. Pestering is excessive. Know the line. Walk it with confidence.

If you're nervous but you pressed send anyway, that's a win. If this chapter left you feeling braver or more willing to pitch yourself, you're already on your way. Your story is worth telling.

Pitchworthy Power Move

Write three versions of the same pitch angle:

1. For a national glossy
2. For a local news outlet
3. For a niche podcast

This exercise will force you to flex your story across formats, and prep you to pitch smarter, faster, and more effectively.

PR Myth You Can Ditch

"If you send one pitch and don't hear back, it means they're not interested."

Nope. They're busy. Or didn't see it. Or it wasn't the right time. Follow up. Then pitch again later with a fresh angle. Real visibility takes real persistence.

Pitchworthy Prompt

What story does your brand tell *right now* that would make a journalist say, "Oh, this is different"?

Now write that pitch's subject line.

CHAPTER **10**

Newsworthy News Releases

There's a reason news releases have been around since the early 1900s. And no, it's not because PR people hate change.

It's because, when done right, a news release is one of the most efficient, accessible, and underestimated ways to tell the world what you're doing—and why it matters.

Stop sending fluff, start sending stories worth printing.

Sure, the format is old school. But the opportunity? Still major.

And yet, every time I bring up news releases to a client, they flinch.

"Aren't press releases dead?"

"No one reads those anymore, right?"

"Isn't that what you use when you don't know what else to do?"

Wrong. Wrong. And very wrong.

The news release is alive and well, and in the right hands, it's a credibility goldmine.

This chapter is your guide to writing one that doesn't just check a box, but actually creates buzz, builds trust, and gets noticed.

What Even *Is* a News Release?

Let's clarify. A news release (also called a press release or media release) is an official brand announcement written for public distribution.

It's meant to inform journalists, stakeholders, and customers of something newsworthy: a launch, a milestone, an award, an event, a major update.

Think of it as your *formal* pitch, less personal than a direct media email, but still packed with potential. It's the announcement version of your "I'm not messing around" voice.

Typically one page (two max), a news release gives journalists everything they need to write a story *without* having to chase down additional context, quotes, or info.

But don't get it twisted: You're not writing ad copy. You're writing for a time-starved journalist who needs the facts, fast. And it has to be something that's actually newsworthy.

No: "We redesigned our packaging!"

Yes: "We partnered with Lululemon to launch a limited-edition wellness line featured in *Vogue*."

See the difference?

The Five Rules of a Pitchworthy Press Release

1. Start With a Headline That Slaps

    This is your hook. Your headline is your first—and sometimes only—shot at making someone care.

    Use clear, compelling language. No fluff. No jargon. And please, for the love of media literacy, no "innovative solutions."

    Keep it under 80 characters. Make it scroll-stopping.

    Example: Instead of "XYZ Corp Announces New Sustainability Initiative," try "XYZ Corp Commits $10M to Carbon-Free Packaging by 2026."

2. Hit the Fives Ws in Your Lead Paragraph

    If your first paragraph doesn't tell us who, what, when, where, and why, you've already lost.

This is not the place to ramble about your founder's childhood dream. This is a news release. Give us the headline-worthy summary right away, then unpack the details later.

3. Add a Quote That Builds the Story

    Every solid press release includes a quote, but not every quote is worth including.

    It should sound human. It should show impact. And it should reflect *why* the news matters.

    Avoid generic filler like, "We're so excited to announce . . ." and aim for something meaningful and specific.

    Think: "This partnership accelerates our mission to eliminate single-use plastic, and gives consumers a real, everyday way to vote with their wallets."

4. Contextualize with Background Info

    Use the third paragraph to zoom out. Add context or color that helps the media understand why this matters in the bigger picture.

    Is this the first time something like this has happened in your industry? Is it tied to a larger cultural trend? This is your chance to connect the dots.

5. Wrap With the "Boilerplate"

    This is your brand's bio in press release form.

    One clean, concise paragraph about who you are, what you do, and where people can learn more. Think of it like a polished About section with a hyperlink.

Plug-and-Play Press Release Template

Use this template as your starting point for crafting a press release that's concise, compelling, and camera-ready.

FOR IMMEDIATE RELEASE
[Insert Today's Date]

Headline:
Write a compelling headline in title case. Make it clear, punchy, and no longer than 80 characters.

Example: "Dallas-Based Design Firm Launches Bold New Kitchen Collection Inspired by Italian Riviera"

Subhead (Optional):
Use this line to provide a bit more context or tease the story angle. Think of this like a tweet: short, smart, and shareable.

Example: "Launch marks the brand's first international-inspired line, blending timeless elegance with functional luxury."

[City, State] – [Date] — Start strong by answering the Five Ws (who, what, when, where, why) in two to three sentences. This is the media's intro to the story—no fluff, no backstory. Just tell them what's happening and why it matters.

Example: McCroskey Interiors today announced the debut of its latest kitchen collection, Amalfi, inspired by summer living on the Italian coast. The line combines bold color palettes with clean-lined cabinetry and will be available exclusively through designer showrooms beginning November 1.

Insert a quote from a founder or key spokesperson here.
Make it sound natural, emotional, and purposeful, not robotic.

Example: "We wanted to create something that felt fresh and fearless," said Laura McCroskey, founder and lead designer. "This collection brings a little bit of la dolce vita into the heart of the home."

Add a second paragraph that provides context or significance. This is your chance to zoom out. Tie the news into a trend, explain how it fits into your larger brand vision, or show how it solves a problem.

Example: The Amalfi Collection comes at a time when luxury homeowners are embracing maximalist color, nostalgic travel references, and ultra-functional design. McCroskey Interiors is known for anticipating trends before they break—and designing spaces that don't just look good but work beautifully.

Optional second quote or final thought. If you have a second spokesperson (or an external partner/retailer), include a quote here. Otherwise, summarize the story with one final call to action or insight.

About [Your Brand Name]

This is your boilerplate. One paragraph, max. Include your brand name, what you do, where you're based, and what you're known for. Keep it tight and hyperlink your website.

Example: McCroskey Interiors is a luxury design studio based in Kansas City, specializing in bold, livable interiors that reflect the personality of every client. Known for its fearless use of color, layered styling, and functional elegance, the firm's work has been featured in *Architectural Digest, Rue,* and *House Beautiful.* Learn more at www.mccroskeyinteriors.com.

Media Contact:
[Name]

[Email]
[Phone number]
[Website]
[Social handles (if relevant)]

When to Use a Press Release
(And When to Just . . . Don't)

News releases are most effective when they actually announce something. Here are a few scenarios where a release is warranted:

- You're launching a new product or service.
- You're opening a new store, studio, or HQ.
- You've secured funding, landed a partnership, or won a major award.
- You're hosting a newsworthy event or pop-up.
- You've rebranded and want to formally introduce your new identity.

Skip the release when:

- You're simply updating your website.
- You're doing a routine internal promotion.
- You're launching a low-stakes sale.

Not everything is press release material, and that's okay. Choose your moments.

News Release Versus Pitch: What's the Difference?

If you're thinking, *Wait, didn't I already pitch this to the media?*—great question.

Here's the rule:

A *pitch* is a personalized note that tees up a story idea. A *news release* is an official announcement, written like a news story. The pitch leads with relevance. The news release delivers the details.

In practice? You often use both. You pitch your top media contacts directly, and include the news release as a resource.

Think of it as the show pony (pitch) and the workhorse (release) working together.

Distribution That Actually Gets You Coverage

So you've written a killer release. Now what?

This is where most people fall flat. Distribution *matters* just as much as the writing.

Here's how to make sure your release gets seen:

1. Send to your curated media list first.

    Don't blast. Strategically send to your best-fit media contacts via email. Include a short, customized note and paste the release in the body of the email (no attachments, please).

2. Use wire services sparingly and strategically.

    Platforms like PRWeb, Business Wire, or GlobeNewswire can amplify your reach, but they aren't magic. Use them for investor news, big partnerships, or national campaigns—not every sale or product drop.

3. Embargo for insider access.

    Give key contacts early access to your release under embargo (meaning they agree not to publish until a specific date/time). This makes them feel like VIPs and gives them time to prep coverage.

4. Publish on your site.

    Create a press page or newsroom section on your website. That way, you control the narrative, and give future journalists a place to verify and cite your past coverage.

5. Share the coverage.

    When your release gets picked up, don't let the story die there. Share it on social. Send a follow-up email to your list. Tag the journalist. Celebrate it in your newsletter. Your audience can't amplify what they don't see.

Pitchworthy Power Move

Write once; distribute everywhere.

Treat your press release as a multiuse content asset. Post excerpts on LinkedIn. Turn quotes into Reels. Repurpose the stats into a carousel. The story deserves more than one spotlight.

PR Myth You Can Ditch

"Press releases are outdated."

Not when they're well-written, well-timed, and well-distributed. The release isn't dead. Boring releases are. Let yours be newsworthy, or don't send it.

Pitchworthy Prompt

What's something in your business worth announcing, but you've been downplaying it out of fear of "bragging"?

Write the headline of a press release you'd be proud to publish. Don't filter it. Just write it.

CHAPTER 11

PR Tools to Use

We've reached the part of the book where I start to feel a little like Oprah.

You get a PR tool! And you get a PR tool! Everyone gets a PR tool!

The right tech makes PR less grind, more gold.

If you've stuck with me this far, you know I love nothing more than sharing practical, powerful strategies to help you go from "Who's that?" to "Wait, she's everywhere." This chapter is no different.

Within these pages, you'll find a curated collection of my favorite tools and platforms, each one designed to help you secure media hits, track your coverage, and amplify your brand story. All without hiring a team or shelling out thousands.

Because here's the thing: PR shouldn't be a gatekept game for the well-connected or well-funded. You just need the right toolkit. And now you've got it.

Source of Sources (SOS)

Created by the original founder of Help a Reporter Out (HARO), Source of Sources is an online platform that delivers real-time media opportunities straight from journalists actively working on deadline.

Twice a day, SOS emails press requests from reporters looking for expert sources. You can filter by category and respond immediately when your brand fits the bill.

You'll often find journalists from outlets like *Forbes*, *Real Simple*, *Fast Company, and O Magazine* actively seeking insights—today. Not someday.

Pro tip: Set aside 20 minutes a day to scan and respond to SOS requests. I've had clients land dream press this way. It works.

sourcesofsources.com

OnePitch

OnePitch is like a dating app for PR, except it actually works.

You submit your pitch once, and the platform matches it to journalists who've opted in to hear about your niche. Every day, reporters receive a curated email filled with stories they actually want to write.

You stay in control the entire time. You write the pitch. You control what's submitted. And only the journalists who are prescreened to care about your topic see it.

It's the opposite of cold pitching, and a game changer for brands who want to be selective and strategic.

onepitch.co

Featured

Think Forbes Councils meets Quora, minus the monthly dues.

Featured flips the traditional PR process by putting the journalist's questions front and center. You browse real-time editorial queries from top-tier media and contribute quick, quotable responses.

It's the easiest way to get quoted and build backlinks to your website—without ever writing a full pitch or press release.

The platform also lets you claim a personal profile to track your quotes, get credit, and share your wins.

featured.com

Podpitch

If podcast guesting is part of your visibility strategy (and it should be), Podpitch is your new best friend.

It's a streamlined booking and pitching service that helps experts like you land guest spots on top-ranking shows, without having to research hosts or send dozens of cold emails.

You can browse open podcast guest requests, pitch yourself directly, or even have Podpitch do it for you. The best part? Hosts on the platform are actively looking for guests, which means no more unanswered DMs or awkward outreach.

Perfect for founders who are ready to be heard and not just seen.

podpitch.com

Anewstip

Google is great . . . until it isn't.

When you need to track down the journalist who covered your competitor—or find someone who's tweeted about your industry 47 times this week—Anewstip delivers.

It allows you to search millions of media mentions, tweets, and article archives by keyword. You can filter by date, relevance, language, and more.

It also includes influence scores and contact details for most reporters. Meaning? You can build a media list and see what each person actually covers before you pitch.

anewstip.com

Google Alerts

This one's simple but essential.

Set up alerts for your name, business, product, and even your competitors. It's how you'll know when you're mentioned (or misquoted), what's being said about you online, and when a journalist mentions your topic of expertise.

Plus, it's free and only takes 60 seconds to set up.

google.com/alerts

Dropbox or Google Drive

Journalists won't open attachments. Period.

That's why your media kit, headshots, press releases, and B-roll need to live in the cloud. Use Dropbox or Google Drive to house your assets, and share a tidy, organized link whenever someone needs visuals or background info.

Pro tip: Create one master folder for your brand with subfolders labeled "Images," "Press Release," "About," "Boilerplate," and "Quotes." Keep it polished, keep it light, and update quarterly.

Staffbase

Curious whether your dream editor opened your pitch? Want to know if that follow-up email actually landed?

Staffbase is my go-to tool for email tracking. It lets you see when someone opens your message and offers a free plan that covers 10 tracked emails per day.

You also can use it to schedule pitches in advance, so your email hits inboxes at just the right time (like Tuesday morning, 9:37 a.m.— chef's kiss).

staffbase.com

Publicity Practice

Ready to get scrappy and start pitching like a pro? Choose two tools from this chapter and start using them this week.

Use Anewstip to search journalists who've covered your competitors. Set up a Google Alert for your name and brand. Pitch a podcast host via Podpitch. Try OnePitch or SOS and respond to an active media request.

Remember, these are free for a reason: You're not paying in dollars, but in time. So block an hour, roll up your sleeves, and treat this like the visibility sprint it is.

The right tools won't do your PR for you. But they'll make it a whole lot easier, and a lot more fun.

Pitchworthy Power Move

Block 30 minutes on your calendar every Monday to check Source of Sources, OnePitch, and Podpitch. Create a reusable pitch template for fast replies, and treat it like your standing PR workout. Consistency is what separates the darlings from the wishful thinkers.

PR Myth You Can Ditch

"You need an expensive PR firm to get major coverage."

Nope. You need Google Alerts, a solid pitch, and tools like Featured or Anewstip. Your effort, *not* your budget, is what moves the needle.

Pitchworthy Prompt

Which two tools from this chapter will you commit to using this week? Why those two? What would visibility in your dream outlet do for your brand right now?

CHAPTER 12

Perfect Press Pages

B efore we dive in, let's make one thing clear: If you've ever landed press—or plan to—you need a press page. Full stop.

A thoughtfully built press page is like your brand's VIP lounge: a curated, high-touch experience where editors, podcasters, influenc-

Your digital first impression better be ready for its close-up.

ers, and collaborators can quickly get everything they need to feature you. When done right, it's an always-on publicist working behind the scenes while you sleep.

And the best part? You can create one without extra budget, fancy developers, or special software. This chapter will walk you through exactly what to include, why it matters, and how to make it irresistible, even if your site is built on Squarespace or duct tape.

What Is a Press Page?

A press page (sometimes called a "media kit," "press kit," or "press room") is a dedicated section of your website that acts as a hub for press-related materials.

It's part calling card, part authority flex, part convenience portal.

It houses your most relevant press mentions, high-res photos, downloadable logos, bios, links, and anything else a journalist or content creator might need to tell your story with clarity and ease.

If you've been featured in a podcast, profiled in an outlet, received an award, or are actively pitching, you need a press page. This isn't fluff. It's a friction-reducer for reporters who are short on time but big on deadlines.

Why It Matters

Imagine this: You've just wrapped a killer podcast interview, and the host says they want to include your bio and photo in the show notes. Do you want to fumble through email threads trying to attach a headshot? Or do you want to send one link that has everything neatly organized, updated, and ready to grab?

That's the power of a press page.

More than just convenient, a press page:

- Signals you're media-ready. It tells journalists you know the game, and how to play it.
- Elevates your perceived credibility. Organized equals authoritative.
- Eliminates back-and-forth. It reduces your chance of getting cut from a story because someone couldn't track down your assets.
- Drives organic exposure. The more media-friendly your site, the more likely you'll get linked and quoted.

Don't think of this as extra. Think of it as foundational.

What to Include

The goal here is to balance professionalism with personality. You want this page to feel high-touch, but still true to your voice and visual identity.

At a minimum, your press page should include:

1. Contact Info

    Obvious, but often overlooked. List a clear point of contact for media requests. This can be your publicist (if you have one), your assistant, or you. Don't hide it behind a form.

Include:

Name

Email

Optional: Phone number or Calendly link if you're open to interviews

2. Media Mentions

    This is where you let your features shine. Whether it's a quote in *Business Insider* or a shoutout on a niche podcast, showcase the range of your credibility.

    Use recognizable outlet logos and hyperlink them directly to the original story, article, or episode.

    Pro tip: Avoid the temptation to just say, "As Seen In . . ." with a row of logos, unless they link to something real. It's not just bad practice, it's a trust killer.

3. Approved Bio(s)

    Include a few versions:

    - Short bio (50 words): Perfect for quick reference and social platforms
    - Medium bio (150 words): Great for podcasts and online features
    - Long bio (300+ words): For speaker kits, panels, and in-depth profiles

    Write in third person, keep them updated, and pepper in credibility markers like awards, press features, brand clients, or certifications.

4. Headshots

   At least two to three professional, high-resolution images. Provide both horizontal and vertical options. Bonus points for lifestyle shots, speaking photos, or in-action brand visuals.

   Make them downloadable—no password or permission required.

5. Brand Assets

   Logos (light and dark versions), product photos, founder photos, and any visual media that represents your brand. Group them in organized folders labeled "Headshots," "Logo Variations," "Product Photography," etc.

   Tools like Dropbox or Google Drive work beautifully; just make sure links stay live and updated.

6. Press Releases or Announcements

   Include your most recent press releases or media announcements. If you've launched something new, rebranded, received funding, opened a location, or expanded your team—this is the place to archive it.

7. Speaking Topics or Media Angles

   Make it easy for podcasters and producers to say yes. Include three to five suggested topics you can speak on, plus a few sample questions. This signals that you're not just press-ready—you're pitch-perfect.

Nice-to-Have Extras

Depending on your brand and bandwidth, consider adding:

- Social links or follower count highlights
- A downloadable one-sheet

- Client logos or testimonials
- A short video introduction or media sizzle reel
- A press calendar or availability for interviews/events

Remember, your press page isn't a digital junk drawer. Keep it current, curated, and aligned with your overall brand.

Examples That Do It Well

Need a little inspiration? These three brands each take a distinct but equally Pitchworthy approach to their press pages. Study them closely, then make your own page feel just as intentional.

Calendly: Sleek, Functional, Press-Ready

Calendly's press page is a masterclass in minimalism and utility. True to the brand's promise of simplicity and seamless scheduling, the layout is clean, intuitive, and unmistakably modern. A deep navy-blue header houses two no-fluff calls to action (CTAs)—"Download Media Kit" and "Make a Media Inquiry"—positioning Calendly as both approachable and well-prepared for media attention.

Below that, sections are neatly categorized: press releases, company news, and third-party coverage from outlets like *Forbes, VentureBeat,* and *Fast Company.* It's functional, fast-loading, and designed for one thing—media access without the hunt. In other words, a journalist's dream.

Fenty Beauty: Editorial- and Influencer-Driven

Fenty Beauty flips the traditional press page script. Instead of just showcasing static brand assets, the Fenty team treats influencers like an extension of their in-house media arm. Tutorials, product reviews, and real-world testimonials sit front and center, giving the press (and public) a candid, highly visual look at how the brand lives in the wild.

The takeaway? If your brand relies on community influence, let your fans do the talking. But this move only works if your customer experience is polished, your product delivers, and your visual assets feel editorial—not amateur.

Luvvie Ajayi Jones: Bold, Branded, and Undeniably Her

Luvvie's media page is a Pitchworthy icon. It's crisp, it's colorful, and it's completely aligned with her brand voice: bold, witty, and direct. Assets are easy to find, and her bios, speaking topics, and images are clearly categorized—making it simple for podcast hosts, journalists, and event organizers to find exactly what they need.

This is how you infuse personality without losing professionalism.

What Not to Do

There's a reason most press pages get ignored: They're either outdated, unhelpful, or an aesthetic crime scene. Don't let yours be one of them.

Here are the most common press page pitfalls, and how to avoid them:

No Clear Contact Info

If the media has to *search* for a way to reach you, they'll skip you. Full stop. Don't bury your email under three dropdowns or use a generic "Contact Us" form that lands in a black hole.

Do this instead: Put a real name and direct email front and center. Bonus points if it's labeled "Media Contact."

Dead Links and Dusty Mentions

That feature from 2016? Irrelevant. That broken link to your old head-shot? Embarrassing. Outdated press pages tell journalists your story is stale.

Do this instead: Audit quarterly. Keep logos, articles, bios, and assets fresh and functioning.

Too Much Text, Too Little Value

We don't need your life story in six paragraphs. We need a two-sentence bio, a clean headshot, and a link to your last interview.

Do this instead: Think like a journalist by providing scan-friendly headers, clear sections, and bite-sized content that's easy to quote.

No Visual Assets

If there's no image, there's no story. Editors won't chase you down for photos. If they can't download a high-res headshot or product shot, you've lost the opportunity.

Do this instead: Include a media kit folder with everything they'd need to run a full feature, including photos, logos, product imagery—even social handles.

Press Page FAQs: Quick Answers, Big Impact

Q: Can I just use a Linktree instead of a press page?
A: Nope. A Linktree (or similar tool) is fine for social media bios, but it's not a substitute for a professionally curated press page on your own website.

Why? Because editors, producers, and brand partners want a one-stop destination *you control*, with context, visuals, and credibility cues all in one place. A Linktree says "influencer." A press page says "authority."

Q: Do I really need high-res images?
A: Yes, yes, and yes. Journalists are busy, and they don't have time to chase down visuals. Including high-res, downloadable headshots and brand images (with clear usage rights) on your press page makes their job easier and makes you more likely to get featured.

Bonus points if you include a landscape and portrait version, as well as color and black-and-white options.

Q: What if I haven't had press yet?

A: Use your press page to show you're press-ready. Include a killer bio, downloadable images, brand facts, and a note that you're available for interviews or collaborations.

You'll look polished and proactive—which editors love.

Q: How often should I update it?

A: Every time you get a new feature, win an award, or change your core messaging. Set a reminder to review quarterly so it always reflects your most relevant, reputable self.

Pitchworthy Power Move

Treat your press page like a concierge desk. Make everything easy, elegant, and grab-and-go. Include a "Last Updated" line to show the media your page is current. And don't forget to test your links regularly.

PR Myth You Can Ditch

"You don't need a press page until you're famous."

Truth: You build credibility by *looking* ready for visibility. Even if you've never had press before, you can still build a beautiful, media-ready page. Editors will assume you've got the goods, even if they're the first to write about you.

Pitchworthy Prompt

Make a list of everything a journalist would need to feature you: bios, photos, links, stats, press hits, contact info. Now open your website. Is all of that there and accessible within one click?

If not, schedule an hour this week to map out your page or polish your existing one. It doesn't have to be perfect. It just has to be present.

CHAPTER 13

Promoting Your PR

N ow that we have your press page dialed in and you're poised for greatness, it's time we had a chat about the best way to publicize your media placements.

Don't just land the hit, leverage it everywhere.

How?

By using tips and tricks to help extend your 15 minutes of fame through engaging and fun content.

Because, congratulations! You were just featured in the media. So now what do you do?

Well, once you've received media coverage, it's time to promote your own PR.

Toot Your Horn

I can almost hear you saying, "But wait, KJ. What does that even mean?"

It means it is time to extend your 15 minutes of fame in a strategic way to further your brand recognition. It also is an exercise in making your media coverage work its hardest for you.

While it might sound complicated, promoting your own PR is actually very easy.

For instance, I was recently featured on a podcast discussing PR tips for influencers and bloggers.

Using this example as a guide, I want to talk you through six examples of how you can promote your PR.

Get Social

First, you need to get social. You can do this by promoting the article, mention, or feature across all your social media accounts.

That's right, no matter which platform or channel it is, share from your personal, business, brand, and even your dog's social media accounts.

What's great about this activity is that you can post that day, the following day, or even weeks later.

In fact, if you follow me on Instagram (hint: @kjblattenbauer), you know that I love to share any media opportunity from every account and angle available to me.

Hey, if you can't toot your own horn, who's going to toot it for you?

Remember, being featured in the media isn't just a one-off occurrence. It's evergreen content that keeps on giving and will always be relevant to your audience.

Now and years from now.

And, as you'll remember from a previous chapter, evergreen content is pretty amazing to have at your disposal, isn't it?

Plus, for you shy folks, it's not really bragging if you're merely sharing the kind of word-of-mouth praise others have said about you.

Now is it?

I can almost see you nodding in agreement while you're reading this.

Blog It Out

Another way to extend your 15 minutes of fame is to write about it.

Let's face it, people are busy. Not everyone who loves your brand is going to see every post about you. Likewise, not everyone remembers everything they only read once.

Repetition is key. So be repetitive. See what I did there?

Draft a blog post about the experience of being featured. Include the link to the media you've received. If possible, include an image of your product or brand being featured.

You don't have to be super creative or go crazy here. The point is just to reshare.

Guess what? You're currently reading a chapter in a book that is promoting the media hit I was recently featured in right now.

See how easy that was to promote my own PR?

Talk It Out

Another way to stretch your 15 minutes of fame? Talk about it.

Let's be honest, people are more likely to tune in while they're driving, working out, or folding laundry than to sit down and read a blog. Not everyone catches every post about you and, let's face it, most people don't remember what they only skimmed once.

That's why repetition matters. So repeat yourself. Say it again. Then say it somewhere else.

Record a podcast episode—or guest on someone else's—sharing the story of your media feature. Talk through what it meant for your brand, your clients, or your bigger mission. Mention the outlet, reference the experience, and link listeners back to the feature in your show notes.

You don't need studio-level creativity here. The point is simply to reshare in a new format.

Guess what? If I recorded this very chapter as a podcast, I'd be extending the PR hit of being featured in my own book.

See how easy it is to promote your own PR out loud?

Give Thanks

You know the saying "Gratitude is the right attitude"? It holds true in promoting your PR too.

The same manners you were taught about sending a handwritten thank-you note after an interview or meeting also apply to media coverage and brand love.

Make sure you send a kind note or thank you to the editor you worked with.

And, where appropriate—which is everywhere—copy or tag the source who helped you secure this media coverage or featured you.

I go out of my way to tag and mention those who helped by giving me brand love everywhere it is possible.

This not only helps give them the warm fuzzies but also encourages them to reshare your post or mention. Which, in turn, gets you in front of more people.

Aren't you thankful this type of kindness is the publicity gift that keeps on giving?

Page Yourself

Where do you direct almost every one of your customers or potential customers? To your website!

Does your site have a press page section for you to feature your media coverage, press hits, or features with a note that says "As Seen In . . ."?

It should.

I mean, it is the entire purpose of this part of this book, right?

In fact, you should update your site every time one of your offerings or your brand is featured. And, if you're featured multiple times in one day on a station, include a link to every single clip!

There is no shame in your press page game. Nor is there such a thing as press page overkill.

Trust me on this.

Again, I can't stress this enough: The reality of the situation is, if you aren't promoting yourself, no one else will.

Get a press page on your website today!

Spread the Word

Finally, you need to spread the word.

You know that email list you've spent so much time building?

The day after you secure media coverage is the perfect time to reach out to the fans, followers, and friends on your list.

Send out an email blast to customers, potential clients, wholesalers, and other contacts with the news.

Include the direct link to the article, image, or video when you can.

Make it easy for those on your list to share your exciting news by including a sample tweet or post, or by forwarding on your email in its entirety.

It's not spamming anyone if they've opted in to your mailing list. They signed up because they want to hear from you and are big fans of yours.

Give the people what they're asking for! Send. That. Email.

Alert the Media

Finally, I don't care how big your brand is, when a celebrity wears, uses, or endorses you, it's a big deal.

Alert the media!

Literally, I'm begging you to let the media know, okay?

If a celebrity is photographed wearing or using your product, and that photograph shows up in one of the many celebrity weeklies or celeb style blogs, it's possible for the image to receive millions of views. The level of public interest can, though not always, have a significant, immediate impact on sales.

Get your hands on that photograph (include proper photo credit always) and promote this publicity the same way you would a news article or TV segment using the tips above.

Send a short pitch, featuring this celebrity sighting to your media connections. Particularly those with a celebrity focus.

Don't forget to also send the image to current wholesalers and potential retailers. They like to see the reach your brand can get too.

And tell your customers about it. Whether via your email list or on social media. When a celebrity is repping your brand, others want to rep the exact same thing.

And you don't hate making sales, now do you?

What Not to Do

Let's make sure your PR wins don't get wasted.
Here are a few all-too-common mistakes you'll want to avoid:

- Only posting once, and only to Stories (it disappears in 24 hours!)
- Forgetting to link the article on your website or press page
- Not thanking the journalist or editor publicly

- Uploading a screenshot without context or caption
- Waiting too long to share (relevance fades fast)
- Posting a blurry image of a print story with no link or mention of where to find it

In PR, silence isn't strategic. Share your wins. Loudly and often.

Anatomy of a Caption That Converts

Want to know what makes a media mention post perform? Use this caption framework to draw attention, add value, and build trust:

Hook: Start with excitement, like "Big news!" or "Feeling honored to be featured in . . ."

Backstory: Share what the coverage means or what it represents (Example: "After two years of building this business, seeing it recognized by [outlet] is a full-circle moment.")

CTA: Invite action with a call to action like "Read the article," "Tag someone who needs this," or "Drop a [emoji of choice] if you've been following the journey."

Template: "So thrilled to be featured in [Outlet] talking all things [topic]! This journey has been [brief insight]. Check it out at the link in bio or story highlight! #pressfeature #prwin"

Internal Promotion Counts Too

Your audience isn't just external, it's also your internal team, collaborators, and network. Here's how to promote a press hit internally:

- Announce it on Slack or Teams with a short message and link.
- Add it to your LinkedIn and Instagram bio ("As Seen In . . .").
- Share with investors or donors via a casual update email.
- Mention it in alumni or community groups to generate buzz.

Good PR builds external credibility and internal pride.

Leverage Press for Partnerships

A feature in *Forbes* or mention on *Good Morning America* doesn't just build awareness, it opens doors.

Use it as a reason to:

- Reconnect with potential brand collab partners
- Introduce yourself to podcast hosts or affiliate managers
- Show wholesale buyers your buzz
- Secure new speaking engagements or workshop invites

Email Template: "Hello [Name], I was recently featured in [Outlet] speaking about [Topic]. It made me think of your brand/podcast/event, and I'd love to connect about ways we might collaborate. Here's the link: [URL]"

Highlight Your Highlights

Create a system to showcase your wins consistently.

Here's how:

- Create an "In the Press" Instagram Story Highlight and update it monthly.
- Compile a "Q1 Press Roundup" carousel on Instagram or LinkedIn.
- Add a Media Hits section to your next quarterly investor or board deck.
- Build a running Google Doc with links for internal reference or use in pitch decks.

Your future pitches will thank you.

Pitchworthy Prompt

Which past media hits haven't you fully leveraged? Who could benefit from seeing this coverage, or your potential clients, partners, or team? How will you promote your next PR win across three different channels?

Publicity Practice

Let's make one thing clear: Publicity doesn't promote itself.

Visibility isn't just earned, it's maximized. The moment you land media coverage, you've opened a door. But it's how you walk through it that determines whether people remember your name or forget you by lunch.

So here's your move:

1. Choose one recent press hit, even a podcast guest spot or quote in an article, and map out how you'll promote it using at least *three* of the methods in this chapter.
2. Draft a visibility checklist you can reuse every time you're featured:

   - Did you post it socially?
   - Blog it?
   - Email it?
   - Add it to your press page?
   - Thank and tag the source?
   - Turn it into a talking point for your next pitch?

3. Set a reminder to re-promote that same coverage again in 30 days. (Because once isn't enough, and evergreen stories deserve a second life.)

4. Bonus points if you track engagement or DMs that stem from it. That's data you can use in future pitches, and proof that your publicity works.

You didn't do all that PR work just to *hope* people saw it. Make it impossible to miss.

CHAPTER **14**

Media Kit Magic

Pop quiz time: What's the number one thing that will make you stand out to potential collaborators and the media alike?

Two words: media kit.

Whether you're a fresh-faced founder, a mid-stage maven, or a seasoned PR powerhouse, a polished media kit isn't optional, it's your power move. Done right, it opens doors, seals deals, and positions you as someone worth betting on.

From crickets to collabs, your media kit is the difference.

Let's be real. Media kits aren't rocket science, but they *are* strategic. That's the sweet spot this chapter will guide you to.

And I promise, the return on effort here is massive.

What Is a Media Kit, Really?

At its core, a media kit is your brand's calling card.

It's your digital handshake. Your all-in-one "Nice to meet you, let's work together."

But more than that, it's a press-ready file that includes everything someone needs to write about you, partner with you, or share your story with minimal back-and-forth.

That's power.

Why Media Kits Matter

For influencers? A media kit is your sponsorship resume.

For brands? It's your first impression to journalists, collaborators, and partners.

A well-crafted media kit:

- Saves time by anticipating questions and supplying answers
- Establishes credibility through visuals, stats, and social proof
- Shows you're professional and worth their time

Bottom line? A media kit makes you easy to say yes to.

What to Include in a Brand Media Kit

At a minimum, include the following in your media kit:

- A news-style press release or brief brand bio
- High-resolution logo and product images
- A few founder quotes or executive bios
- Recent press hits (within six months, max)
- Contact info (email and phone)
- Social media handles
- Company milestones or timeline
- Stats: revenue growth, team size, locations, customer reach

Optional extras: video walkthrough, testimonials, B-roll footage, downloadable media folders.

What to Include in an Influencer Media Kit

Different flavor, but same purpose. Here's what to include in an influencer media kit:

- A standout headshot or personal brand photo collage
- 100-word (or less) bio about you and your platform

- A short blurb about your audience (who they are, why they follow)
- Stats: unique monthly visitors, followers, email list, engagement rate
- Your content services (e.g., sponsored posts, giveaways, user-generated content, events)
- Clear pricing
- Collab history and testimonials
- Contact info and links

Pro Tip: Keep it current. Refresh quarterly. And if a number doesn't serve you? Leave it out.

Design and Delivery

Yes, looks matter. Use tools like Canva or Adobe Express, or hire a designer to create a layout that reflects your aesthetic.

Keep it to one to two pages, tops. PDF it. And make sure it's easily downloadable from your website.

Common Media Kit Mistakes to Avoid

Let's not sabotage our spotlight moment.

Mistake: Using outdated stats
Fix: Add "Updated [Month Year]" to your stat section.

Mistake: No pricing or vague rates
Fix: Be transparent or offer ranges. Saves everyone time.

Mistake: No contact info
Fix: Always include a dedicated PR or media inquiry contact.

Mistake: Dull design that looks like a tax document
Fix: Use visuals and brand colors to tell your story.

Mistake: Trying to include *everything*
Fix: Think curated, not cluttered.

Sample Intro Snippet for Your Media Kit

Here's a polished plug-and-play template for a compelling opener:

About [Your Name or Brand]

[Name] is a [short but specific descriptor, e.g., "Dallas-based interior designer and author"] who helps [ideal client] achieve [result].

Featured in [top three outlets], [first name] is known for [noteworthy trait or signature work].

With a community of over [#] loyal followers and a proven record of success, [she/he/they] bring creativity, strategy, and media-ready moments to every collaboration.

Real Brand Media Kits to Inspire

Want a little inspiration before you dive in? Here are a few standout media kits from real brands doing it right:

1. Glossier

   Minimal. Branded. Perfectly aligned with their aesthetic. Glossier's media assets hub provides high-res logos, product images on white, and stylized shots that editors love. It's proof that simplicity, when done well, speaks volumes.

2. Airbnb

   The Airbnb press room functions like an editorial destination. Not only does it offer media kits and fact sheets for each program or campaign, but it includes executive bios, recent press coverage, and an organized digital asset manager. The takeaway? Think like a newsroom.

3. Fenty Beauty

   Fenty's media center highlights its commitment to inclusivity, with high-impact visuals, social proof (including influencer content), and easy-to-navigate categories. The takeaway here is vibe. Make your press materials feel like your brand.

4. Luvvie Ajayi Jones

Her press page feels like an extension of her voice—bold, clear, no fluff. Her bio, media mentions, downloadable head-shots, and speaking topics are easy to find and use. And that personality-packed tone? Chef's kiss.

Design Tips That Make a Difference

Your media kit doesn't need to be designed by a *Vogue* layout editor, but presentation still matters. A few simple rules:

- Use your brand colors and fonts. It should visually match your website, email signature, and social feed.
- Break it up. Use bold headers, bullet points, and visuals to keep readers engaged.
- Keep it to one page, max, front and back. Short, clean, and skimmable wins the race. If you absolutely must include more, use hyperlinks to extended materials hosted online.
- Save it as a PDF. Always. Every time.

How to Use Your Media Kit in the Wild

What good is having a stellar media kit if it just sits in your Google Drive? Here's when and how to use it:

- Attach it to your pitch emails (when relevant).
- Include a "Download Our Media Kit" button on your press page.
- Link it in your email signature.
- Send it to event organizers or podcast hosts ahead of interviews.
- Include it when you apply for features, awards, or partnerships.
- Use excerpts from it on your About page or speaking bio.

Remember, you don't have to explain everything in an email pitch if your media kit does the heavy lifting for you.

Plug and Play Pitch Copy

Here's a sample email to help you get started using your media kit in outreach:

> Subject: Introducing [Your Name or Brand Name] – Media Kit Inside
>
> Hello [Name],
>
> I wanted to introduce myself and share a bit about [Your Brand or Business Name]. We're doing exciting work around [brief positioning statement or media angle], and I think it could be a great fit for your audience.
>
> I've attached our media kit here, which includes a bio, recent press, images, and story angles.
>
> If this sparks your interest, I'd love to talk further or explore how we might collaborate.
>
> Thanks so much for considering,
>
> [Your Name]
> [Website]
> [Contact Info]
> [Socials]

Keep this saved in your Notes app. Use it often.

Audit Accordingly

Answer these to help clarify what belongs in your kit (and what doesn't):

- *What do I want the media or potential collaborators to know about me immediately?*
- *What's the first impression I want my headshot and intro paragraph to create?*
- *What's my most compelling recent press or accomplishment?*

- *What makes my brand different, visually or vocally?*
- *Am I including only what's necessary, or overloading my kit with filler?*

Pro tip: Less "Here's everything I've ever done," more "Here's why I'm right for you."

Maintenance Plan: Keep It Fresh

Even the best media kit needs a little upkeep. Here's your simple review cadence to keep yours updated without taking up too much of your time.

Every three months

- Update stats, pricing (if relevant), and recent press.
- Swap out dated headshots or brand images.

Check links, especially Drive or Dropbox files, to avoid broken access.

Every six months

- Ask for new testimonials.
- Review your bio. Have your offers, services, or angles changed?

Set a recurring calendar reminder. A dusty media kit doesn't get results.

Pitchworthy Power Move

Use your media kit proactively—not reactively.

Attach it to every pitch. Link it in your email signature. Post it on your website. Drop it in DMs. This isn't a "wait to be asked" moment, it's your go-to flex.

PR Myth You Can Ditch

"No one reads media kits."

Wrong. The right people *skim strategically*, and the right kit makes it easy for them to say yes. Don't underestimate the power of packaging.

Pitchworthy Prompt

Spend 30 minutes compiling your key assets:

- Your best photos
- A short founder bio
- Three to five media logos or testimonials
- Updated stats

Open Canva. Choose a sleek template. Drop your assets in, then PDF it.

Boom! You just became someone editors *want* to work with.

CHAPTER 15

Media Mindset

Let's talk about the elephant in the green room:

It's not your website.

It's not your offer.

It's not even your pitch.

Confidence, not contacts, is your strongest PR tool.

It's your mindset.

I know that's not what you expected to hear in a book about PR. But if you've ever sat on a pitch draft for days, talked yourself out of submitting that award, or ghosted an opportunity because you didn't feel "ready," you already know: This isn't a strategy problem.

It's a confidence one.

Before we go another step further, let's get honest about what's really going on when you freeze at the send button or downplay your big moment on Instagram.

This chapter is the bridge between everything you've learned and the bold action that puts it to work.

Let's clear the clutter between your brilliance and the spotlight it deserves.

The Real Reason You're Stalling

I've worked with founders who have built million-dollar empires, and still break into hives at the thought of a camera interview.

Visibility is personal. It feels risky.

And if you've ever thought . . .

- *What if I sound like I'm bragging?*
- *What if they say no?*
- *What if I'm not ready?*
- *What if I go viral for the* wrong *reason?*

. . . You're not alone.

But let's be clear: Hiding helps no one.

Not your clients. Not your mission. Not your bottom line.

The media isn't waiting for perfection. It's waiting for presence.

Let's Talk About Rejection

Rejection is baked into PR.

Not every pitch lands. Not every journalist replies. Not every email even gets opened.

But none of that is personal.

You're not being snubbed. You're being sorted. Your message just didn't fit their content calendar *today*.

That's it. That's all.

Here's the power play: The more consistently you show up, the more likely your name sticks when the right moment *does* come around.

Resilience beats perfection every single time.

Reframe Your Fears

The thing that most people get wrong about visibility fears is that they try to eliminate them. Instead, let's *reinterpret* them.

- Nervous about promoting yourself? That's a sign you care about substance. Good.
- Scared to pitch? That means the opportunity matters. Also good.
- Worried you'll sound like an amateur? That means you're self-aware enough to want to improve. Still good.

Fear is just your brain's way of flagging risk. But risk is the price of recognition. And you're not here to play small.

The Science of Confidence

Confidence isn't a personality trait. It's a skill. And this skill is built through three things:

1. Preparation – Know your message and practice it.
2. Repetition – The more you pitch, post, and press send, the easier it gets.
3. Perspective – Remember that media is just a conversation. And you belong in the room.

Still think you're not ready?

Neither was Brené Brown when she gave her first TEDx talk.

Oprah didn't wait for someone to discover her—she made herself undeniable.

Reese Witherspoon built an entire media empire by backing her own stories when others wouldn't.

They didn't wait to be crowned credible. They claimed it.

You can too.

Make Your Mindset Part of Your Strategy

Media strategy without confidence is just a plan you'll never use.

Here's what to do today:

1. Say your elevator speech out loud.
2. Practice introducing yourself as an expert in your field.
3. Send that pitch you've been sitting on.
4. Screenshot your last press hit and set it as your phone wallpaper.

You're not an imposter. You're an expert learning how to speak up. It's not bragging. It's branding.

Pitchworthy Power Move

Record your elevator speech on your phone's voice memo app. Then listen back.

Does it sound like you? Adjust until it rolls off your tongue. Confidence isn't just about what you say, it's about how it sounds when you say it.

PR Myth You Can Ditch

"You have to wait until you're more established to pitch."

Wrong. Media isn't reserved for "big names." It's for people with something valuable to say.

If you can help someone or offer a new perspective, you're ready.

Pitchworthy Prompt

What visibility fear am I holding onto, and how would I act if I knew I was already the expert?

Write it down. Then go act like it.

Publicity Practice

Confidence can't be outsourced. But it can be built.

This week, do one thing that pushes you outside your comfort zone:

- Introduce yourself at an event as "someone the media should know."
- Submit a pitch that feels slightly out of your league.
- Film a short video introducing who you are and what you do, and post it.

One bold action rewires your brain for the next.

And remember, confidence doesn't come before visibility. It comes *from* it.

CHAPTER 16

When PR Isn't Working

Let's have a heart-to-heart, shall we?

You've crafted the perfect pitch. You've done your research. You hit send with high hopes.

And then? Crickets.

No reply. No feature. No momentum.

Silence isn't failure—it's feedback. Make adjustments and move forward.

At first, you're annoyed. Then discouraged. And finally, you start to wonder: *Maybe I'm just not newsworthy.*

Stop right there.

PR is not always an overnight success story. In fact, most of the media hits you admire came after a long game of refining, reworking, and relentless pitching.

So if your PR efforts feel like they're falling flat, this chapter is here to show you it's not the end—it's just time to reassess, refocus, and reignite.

Let's fix what's actually broken and leave the self-doubt behind.

First: Reframe the "Failure"

Before we dig into strategy, you need to know this:

A pitch that doesn't land isn't a failure. A quiet campaign doesn't mean your brand is broken. And a lack of replies is not a reflection of your worth.

Sometimes it's the timing. Sometimes it's the subject line. Sometimes it's just an editor having a bad day.

So let's remove the shame spiral and start treating PR like what it is: *a process.* Not a slot machine.

Red Flags to Check First

When a PR campaign isn't working, there's usually a reason (and a fix).

Start here:

1. Your messaging is vague. If your pitch reads like a résumé or a marketing brochure, it's probably not clicking with a journalist. You need a *story*, not just a stat sheet.
2. Your media list is off. Are you pitching beauty editors with a fintech founder? Or local news with a product they can't demo? No matter how great your pitch is, if it's going to the wrong inbox, it's dead on arrival.
3. You're pitching too soon. If your brand is still figuring out its niche, a full media blitz may be premature. Nail your messaging, proof of concept, and visuals first.
4. There's no clear angle. "Hello, I exist" isn't a pitch. The media wants hooks, trends, takes, and timeliness. What's the *why now* of your story?
5. You're ghosting after one send. You sent it once. Got no reply. And moved on. No! The follow-up is where the magic happens.

Check Your Timing and Angle

Let's be blunt: Some pitches flop because they're just not timely.
Before you give up, ask yourself:

*   *Is this relevant to what's trending right now?*
*   *Am I anchoring this pitch to an upcoming event, season, or news moment?*
*   *Is there a fresher or more contrarian way to frame this?*

You might just need a headline refresh, not a full rewrite.

Common Campaign Killers

Here are the repeat offenders that quietly sabotage even solid PR efforts:

- Unclear CTA – You didn't tell the journalist exactly what you want. Do you want them to interview you? Feature your product? Include you in a roundup? Spell it out.
- No media assets – You pitched without images, links, or bios. Don't make editors chase down your story; hand it to them on a silver platter.
- Inconsistent follow-through – You pitched once in January and again in . . . July? PR works when it's part of your rhythm, not a once-a-quarter panic blast.
- Pitching without relationship – If you've never engaged with a journalist's work and your pitch is totally cold, your odds drop fast. Warm it up.

Shift Strategy Without Starting Over

If you've hit a wall, here's how to pivot without torching everything:

- Rework your angle – Keep the core of your pitch but lead with a different hook.
- Try a new outlet tier – If national isn't biting, go local. If print is slow, go digital.
- Bundle your pitch – Pitch a story series, a trend report, or a package of experts.
- Pitch a different person at the same outlet – Just make sure it's relevant to their beat.
- Repurpose as content – Didn't land with the press? Turn it into a blog post or LinkedIn article. Your audience still needs to hear it.

Keep Showing Up

Want to know a real PR secret? You only lose when you quit.

Every seasoned PR pro knows that momentum often comes after the third, fourth, or even tenth pitch. The story that gets picked up *now* might be the one you sent six months ago.

Your job is to stay in motion.

- Keep building relationships.
- Keep refining your message.
- Keep showing up with something worth saying.

Because quiet seasons don't mean failure. They mean *you're still in the game.*

Real-Time PR Diagnostics

Here are five questions to ask yourself when you're pursuing PR but only hearing crickets. If your pitches aren't landing—or your features aren't moving the needle—pause and assess with this quick gut check:

1. *Is my pitch clear and specific?*

   Would a stranger know what you're offering and why it matters? If your email feels vague or generic, it's easy to ignore.

2. *Am I targeting the right people?*

   Are you pitching to writers who cover your topic, or just anyone with a media title? A refined media list beats a massive one.

3. *Is the timing aligned?*

   Editors live by editorial calendars. Are you pitching a winter topic in July or a trend piece when everyone's covering breaking news?

4. *Did I follow up strategically?*

If you sent one pitch and ghosted, that's not a campaign, that's a Hail Mary. Follow up with something fresh, not just a "checking in."

5. *Am I solving a problem or just talking about myself?*

Lead with value. Journalists want angles, not bios.

What to Test: Tweak, Don't Trash

Instead of scrapping your whole strategy, experiment with one of these variables:

Element	Test This
Subject Line	Use numbers, urgency, or a curiosity hook.
Outlet	Shift from national to regional, or niche to mainstream.
Timing	Try a different time of day or day of the week.
Angle	Lead with a seasonal tie-in, stat, or contrarian POV.
Visuals	Embed a photo or graphic to catch the eye.
CTA	Make it crystal clear: What do you want the editor to do?

Remember, PR isn't about perfection, it's about persistence, positioning, and playing the long game.

Want to go even deeper with campaign tweaks or need a pitch review? Reach out to me on Instagram at @kjblattenbauer. Let's get it right, together!

Case Study: From Crickets to Coverage

Client: A boutique travel advisor focused on luxury honeymoons.

Original Pitch: "XYZ Travel helps couples plan stress-free honeymoons around the world."

Result: Zero responses after 30-plus cold pitches to lifestyle editors. What wasn't working?

- Too vague – "Stress-free" didn't communicate a newsworthy angle.
- No tie-in to trends or timeliness.
- No personal story or proof of expertise.

The Pivot: We reframed the pitch around the rise in *luxury revenge travel* post-pandemic and led with a stat: "Destination honeymoon bookings are up 47%, and couples are trading cookie-cutter getaways for curated, once-in-a-lifetime itineraries."

We also added a juicy story: The advisor had recently planned a $90,000 honeymoon involving private jet transfers, a Michelin-starred food tour in Tuscany, and a champagne sabering class in the Maldives.

New Result: Within two weeks, the revised pitch landed her features in *Condé Nast Traveler* and *Modern Luxury*.

Lesson: Your pitch can be strong, but still not sticky. A few small tweaks can turn silence into spotlight.

Case Study: Coaching Pitches That Finally Landed

Client: A leadership coach helping women in STEM rise into executive roles.

Original Pitch: "I help women gain confidence and advocate for themselves at work."

Result: Crickets; 40+ pitches, no interest—even from niche business outlets.

What wasn't working?

- Overdone language: "Confidence" and "advocacy" didn't stand out.
- No data or differentiator.
- Pitch was focused on *what* she does, not *why it matters now*.

The Pivot: We flipped the script and reframed her expertise around a timely trend: tech layoffs and retention gaps for women in engineering.

New subject line: "Why mid-career women in STEM are quitting—and how companies can keep them."

We led with a strong stat, added a client story, and positioned her as a go-to expert on gender equity in tech.

New Result: Within 10 days, she was quoted in *Fast Company*, booked on a tech industry podcast, and asked to contribute an op-ed to *Fortune*.

Lesson: Coaches, especially those in saturated spaces, must lean into timely data, real-world results, and contrarian takes. Your message is likely solid, but your framing needs fire.

Pitchworthy Power Move

Ask an editor why your last pitch didn't land. You'd be surprised how many are willing to offer a quick reply, and their feedback could unlock your next feature.

PR Myth to Ditch

"If it didn't work the first time, it means you're not newsworthy."

Absolutely not. It means the pitch wasn't the right fit for *that* outlet *at that time*.

Newsworthiness isn't binary. It's about match, moment, and message.

Pitchworthy Prompt

What's one angle you haven't tried—but truly believe in?

Write the headline. Draft the hook. And send it this week.

Publicity Practice

It's gut check time.

Pull up the last three pitches you sent. For each one, ask:

- *Was it relevant and timely?*
- *Did I offer a clear story, not just an intro?*
- *Did I include a CTA, links, and assets?*
- *Did I follow up?*

If not, fix it and resend.

If yes, and you still got silence, try a new angle or outlet. But do *not* stop.

You're not being ignored. You're being refined. And this is the part of PR that most people aren't brave enough to push through.

You are.

CHAPTER 17

Creating Your Signature Story

Let's get this out of the way: A list of impressive accomplishments doesn't make a great pitch.

It's your story, not the facts, that gets you featured.

What gets journalists to stop scrolling? What earns you a feature instead of a footnote? What makes your audience remember you instead of just being vaguely aware of you?

A signature story.

Your story is more than how you started. It's the emotional glue that makes your brand stick. The thread that connects the audience to your mission. The reason a producer calls *you* instead of someone with the same résumé.

And guess what? You already have that story.

We just need to find it, shape it, and pitch it.

What Is a Signature Story?

A signature story is the heartbeat of your brand.

It's not your whole life history or a rote timeline of achievements. It's the curated, intentional arc that reveals:

- Who you are
- What you believe
- Why you do what you do
- What all this means to your audience

It's what you share in interviews, in keynotes, in bios, and in the first 30 seconds of a pitch.

And when it's crafted well? It makes people lean in and say, "Tell me more."

Four Elements of a Signature Story

All great signature stories follow a clear emotional arc. Here's the anatomy:

1. Origin

    Where did this all begin? What was the moment that sparked your idea or shaped your worldview?

    Think: The uncomfortable truth, the big question, or the personal moment that cracked everything open.

2. Turning Point

    What was the challenge or decision that pushed you forward? The stakes get real here.

    Think: The make-or-break moment, the risk you took, the shift that changed everything.

3. Transformation

    What happened as a result? What changed in you or around you?

    Think: The insight, the pivot, the new way of operating. Show growth.

4. Outcome

    What are you doing now, and for whom? How does your story translate into impact?

    Think: Who benefits because you went through that journey? Where does your audience fit in?

When you connect all four?

You don't just inform. You inspire.

Story Versus Statement

Let's break this down further. Many founders confuse their story with a statement.

A statement says: "We believe in making sustainable products for women who care about the planet."

Fine. But *flat*.

A story says: "When I realized I'd spent 10 years in fast fashion—and contributed to more waste than I care to admit—I knew I had to build something different. I couldn't find the kinds of products I wanted to wear that didn't cost the earth . . . so I started making them."

See the difference?

One informs. The other connects.

And connection wins every single time.

Brand Stories in the Wild

Let's look at a few examples of signature stories that built empires:

SPANX

Sara Blakely's origin story is legendary PR gold.

She cut the feet off control-top pantyhose before a party, felt amazing, and realized no one was making shapewear like this. Her story wasn't just about innovation, it was about *empathy*. She built a billion-dollar brand because she solved a problem *she personally felt*. And she tells that story every chance she gets.

The Lip Bar

Founder Melissa Butler was rejected on *Shark Tank*. That failure became the fuel for her story.

Now she owns shelves in Target and CVS. Her brand is rooted in the idea that beauty shouldn't be dictated by narrow standards, and she tells that story as a badge of boldness.

Patagonia

Their story is centered around activism, not just apparel. They connect their founding narrative with their mission today. It's not just "We sell clothes." It's "We're a company that exists to protect the planet."

And it shows up everywhere—from hangtags to headlines.

Where to Use Your Signature Story

Once you have your signature story, it becomes your greatest asset.

Use it in:

- Media pitches – Anchor your relevance with a clear why. "The reason I started this is . . ." makes it personal and powerful.
- Panel introductions – Don't list your credentials. Open with a moment that shaped your mission.
- Podcast interviews – This is the juicy content hosts are looking for. Lead with story, not self-promo.
- LinkedIn bios and About pages – People remember a great story far more than a long list of accolades.
- Brand decks and media kits – The human side of your brand? That's what gets sponsors and journalists to care.

Pitchworthy Power Move

Record your story as a voice memo, no script. Talk like you're explaining it to a friend. Then transcribe and refine.

The most magnetic stories come from real conversation, not stiff writing.

PR Myth to Ditch

"Journalists only care about credentials."

False. They care about what *makes you different*. Your story is your differentiator. Credentials are just the receipts.

Pitchworthy Prompt

What's the origin moment that made you start this brand, or shift how you work? What did it teach you?

Write out that memory in detail.

Publicity Practice

Time to shape your own signature story.

Try this framework:

1. Origin – What sparked your idea or changed your path?
2. Turning Point – What challenge or moment pushed you forward?
3. Transformation – What did you learn or become?
4. Outcome – Who benefits because of what you created?

Write it once in full. Then tighten it to 150 words. Then boil it down to two to three sentences.

That version?

That's your pitch-ready signature story. And you just became way more media-worthy.

CHAPTER 18

Be a Go-To Media Guest

Getting the yes is only half the job. *How* you show up when the spotlight's on? That's what cements you as a trusted expert, a repeat guest, and a media darling worth remembering.

This is your moment to shift from "interesting idea" to "in-demand guest." To prove you're not just quotable, you're a *resource*.

Getting booked puts you in the room; showing up like a pro makes you unforgettable.

In a world where editors and producers are short on time and high on expectations, nothing is more valuable than someone who's smart, sound bite-ready, and easy to work with.

So whether you're prepping for your first TV spot, a podcast interview, or a keynote panel, consider this chapter your greenroom guide to showing up like the pro you are.

Media 101: Know Your Format

Not all media is created equal. You'll need to tailor your delivery depending on the platform.

Here's the rundown:

TV and Livestream

Short, visual, energetic. Think *big smile, clean background, and punchy quotes.*

Podcasts and Radio

Longer-form, conversational, and rich in storytelling. Share anecdotes, not essays.

Print and Digital

You'll often be quoted selectively. Speak in sharp, self-contained thoughts that can stand alone as pull quotes.

Panels and Live Events

Clarity, confidence, and presence. Be concise, but also warm and engaging. Think, "generous leader," not "know-it-all."

Interview Prep Checklist

Before you go on air, or Zoom, ask yourself:

- *What's the headline takeaway I want listeners/readers/viewers to remember?*
- *What two or three key messages or stories will I repeat or reference?*
- *Do I have a killer stat, surprising insight, or myth to bust?*
- *Am I dressing the part?* (On camera, solids are greater than patterns. Think good lighting. Quiet background. Audio checks.)
- *Do I have a CTA ready, if appropriate?* (Even if it's just "Follow me on Instagram" or "Check out my blog.")
- *Do I know who the outlet serves?* (Tailor your tone and references accordingly.)

Pro tip: Practice answers out loud. Record a voice memo. Soundbites are *spoken* assets, not written ones.

Delivering a Killer Soundbite

Want to get quoted? Make it quotable.
A great soundbite is:

- Short (10–20 seconds)
- Unexpected or contrarian
- Emotionally or intellectually sticky
- Easy to remember or repeat

Instead of: "Well, I think branding is really important in today's competitive market."
Try: "Branding is the difference between getting chosen . . . and getting skipped."
Here's a cheat code: Write your main ideas like you'd write tweets. Tight. Punchy. Visual. Evocative.
Don't be afraid to slow down, pause, and emphasize. Give the audience time to absorb what you just dropped.

Handling Curveballs with Grace

Every media guest eventually faces a tricky moment. Here's how to stay pitch-perfect:
If you get a question you don't love: "That's interesting, and here's what I'd add . . ."
If you get off topic: "That brings up something really important we haven't touched on yet . . ."
If you don't know the answer: "I don't have the numbers in front of me, but I can tell you this from experience . . ."
If you freeze or blank: Breathe. Sip water. Smile. Recenter on one of your key talking points and keep going. You're allowed to be human.
Confidence doesn't mean perfection. Confidence means staying present and grounded—no matter what happens.

Your Virtual Media Studio Setup

Whether it's Zoom, Riverside, or national broadcast, your virtual media setup matters more than you think.

Here's what you need:

- Camera at eye level – Use a laptop stand or books to elevate.
- Natural light or a ring light – Bright, even lighting is key.
- External mic or AirPods – Crisp audio is nonnegotiable.
- Headphones if echo is a risk – Better to look a little tech-y than sound fuzzy.
- Background – Clean, styled, neutral. No clutter. No chaos. Bonus points if it nods to your brand (like a shelf with your book or product).
- On-camera style tips – Solid colors are better than patterns. Avoid all black or all white. Necklines should be higher than usual (scoop necks can disappear on camera). Soft glam wins over full contour.

Turn One Interview into 10 Touchpoints

Great PR content doesn't end with the appearance, it starts there. Here's how to get more mileage out of every single placement:

- Clip highlights from podcasts or videos into 15 to 30 second Reels.
- Create a graphic quote from your soundbite for Instagram.
- Write a blog post expanding on what you shared.
- Email your list with a personal intro and the link.
- Pitch the topic to another outlet with "As seen in . . ." credibility.
- Pin it to your press page for evergreen bragging rights.

Visibility doesn't have to be one-and-done. Make every media moment work overtime.

Pitchworthy Power Move

After your next interview, send a thank-you email that includes a promo plan. Offer to tag the outlet in your posts.

Journalists love guests who help amplify their work.

PR Myth to Ditch

"If you just show up, the interview will go fine."

Wrong.

Great guests are made, not born. They prepare, rehearse, and refine.

Pitchworthy Prompt

Think back to the last time you were interviewed or featured.

- What feedback did you get?
- What did you *wish* you'd done differently?
- What would you repeat or improve next time?

Publicity Practice

Practice makes Pitchworthy.

This week, do a mock interview on your core topic. Record it on video. Watch it back. Take notes. Refine your answers into soundbites.

Even better? Grab a friend and ask them to play "producer." Have them throw you softballs, curveballs, and the occasional curveball disguised as a compliment.

Because when you're pitch-prepped and press-polished? You don't just land interviews. You own them.

CHAPTER 19

Building a Year-Round Visibility Plan

Here's a hard truth: Visibility fades. Not because you're not talented. Not because you're not "newsworthy." But because attention spans are shorter than ever, and the media cycle never sleeps.

Being seen once isn't the same as being remembered.

That's why one of the smartest things you can do as a founder, expert, or creator is stop treating PR like a one-and-done to-do list item . . . and start treating it like the strategic system it is.

Think of this chapter as your PR operating calendar—the plan that ensures your brand stays relevant, visible, and newsworthy year-round.

Let's build it together.

Why One Press Hit Isn't Enough

I've seen it too many times: A founder gets one great press hit—let's say, a glossy magazine feature or an exciting podcast spot—and they celebrate (as they should) . . . but then go radio silent.

They think: *I've made it! I'm set for a while.*

In reality, PR works more like compound interest. The more consistent you are, the more credibility you build. The more credibility you build, the more the media starts coming to you.

This chapter is your invitation to treat PR as a rhythm, not a sprint. A cycle that aligns with your business calendar, your customer's attention span, and your own bandwidth.

How to Tie PR to Your Business Calendar

Before you create any visibility plan, ask yourself this: *What am I selling this year, and when?*

PR should serve the business. Not distract from it.

Your visibility map should align with your internal goals, not just the news cycle.

Ask:

- *When am I launching new offers, products, or campaigns?*
- *When are my peak sales seasons?*
- *When do I typically go quiet, and could PR help fill that gap?*

For example:

- Launching a new course in April? Pitch guest podcast spots on your topic in January.
- Designing a holiday gift guide feature for December? You need to be pitching Christmas near the end of July.
- Opening applications for your retreat in August? Consider a "founder story" feature in June.

Work backward. Give your pitches a lead time of six to eight weeks at minimum. For national publications? Try three to six months.

The Three Visibility Anchors

A year-round PR plan isn't just about press coverage. There are three visibility anchors to rotate between:

1. Media Outreach – This includes traditional pitching, newsjacking, and follow-ups with editors or podcast producers.
2. Platform Building – Your owned media, social, blogs, email, etc., where you control the narrative and create a home base for attention.
3. Community Amplification – Think collaborations, panels, industry awards, affiliate shoutouts, or client spotlights. Earned attention that doesn't come from press, but still boosts your reputation.

When in doubt, cycle through all three each quarter.

PR Checklists

Consistency is the secret sauce. These monthly check-ins make sure your PR game doesn't just spark once—it stays lit.

Your Monthly PR Checklist:

- Check SOS, Qwoted, and podcast callouts weekly.
- Follow up on last month's pitches.
- Share and promote recent media hits across platforms.
- Engage with three to five journalists on social.
- Update your press page or media kit if needed.

Every quarter is your chance to reset the stage by refreshing assets, sharpening angles, and making sure your next big moment is already in motion.

Your Quarterly PR Checklist:

- Map out any launches or campaigns coming up.
- Draft one to three new pitch angles or hooks.
- Refresh key brand assets (headshots, bios, testimonials).
- Check upcoming editorial calendars and awareness dates.
- Book at least one visibility opportunity (interview, event, etc.).

Think of this as tending the fire, so your momentum never dies out.

Leveraging Key Dates and Seasons

Smart PR pros don't just ride trends, they *anticipate* them.
Use cultural moments to ride the wave of relevance. A few examples:

- January – Vision and goal setting; business resolutions
- March – Women's History Month (Hello, female founders!)
- May – Spring home refreshes, graduation, mental health awareness
- July – Summer travel, entrepreneurship, mid-year reflection
- September – Back-to-business, fall interiors, fashion, school prep
- November through December – Holiday gift guides, gratitude, year-end recaps

Grab a big wall calendar. Mark your own brand's key moments. Then layer in editorial opportunities that make sense.
This becomes your visibility blueprint for the year.

Seasonal PR Examples

To make it even more real:

Interior Designers:

- Spring – Organizing trends and refreshes
- Fall – Cozy home must-haves and holiday prep
- Winter – Dream kitchen renovations

Wellness Coaches:

- January – Reset routines
- April – Spring detox features
- August – Back-to-school stress relief tips

Product Brands:

- July – "Christmas in July" gift guide pitching
- November – Black Friday media strategy
- December – Year-end roundup inclusions

Publicity Practice

Establish a Quarterly Pitch Planner and map out:

- One pitch angle per quarter
- One media goal per quarter
- Three people or outlets to reach out to

If you don't have specific campaigns, use seasonal dates to fill in the blanks. If you do? Build visibility around your launch runway.

Pitchworthy Power Move

Look at the next 90 days on your calendar. Where can PR create momentum around what you're already doing?

PR Myth to Ditch

"PR is only for big launches."

Nope. PR is for staying top of mind, even when you're between offers.

Pitchworthy Power Move

Look at the next 90 days on your calendar. Where can PR create momentum around what you're already doing?

CHAPTER 20

How to Handle Negative Press

Your name's finally in the media, but not the way you planned. Maybe a reporter got the facts wrong. Maybe a cranky commenter is calling you a fraud. Or maybe your brilliant idea just didn't land the way you thought it would.

If you're visible long enough, criticism is inevitable.

Here's the truth: If you're visible long enough, criticism is inevitable.

The good news? It's not a career-ender. In fact, how you *respond* is often more memorable than the criticism itself. In this chapter, you'll learn how to manage public perception without spiraling, stalling, or self-sabotaging.

Let's turn down the panic and turn up the PR savvy.

When (and How) to Respond

Not every negative comment warrants a response. But when it does, timing and tone are everything.

Ask yourself:

- *Is this critique factually wrong or just someone's opinion?*
- *Could silence make it worse (or look like guilt)?*
- *Is the criticism gaining traction that could impact my business or brand?*

If it's minor and untrue, it's often better to let it fade. The internet has a short memory. But if it's false *and* spreading, you need to correct the record, calmly and clearly.

"We appreciate the feedback and want to clarify a few important details . . ."

If it's valid, own it. Transparency earns trust. Say what happened, what you've learned, and how you're improving.

"This feedback brought something important to our attention. Here's what we're doing about it . . ."

And if it's a straight-up troll? Don't take the bait. Trolls feed off reaction. Starve them.

Owning the Narrative

The worst thing you can do when criticism hits is freeze.

Visibility means you're in the arena. But staying silent while misinformation spreads allows others to write your story for you. That's not PR, that's panic.

Instead, reclaim your voice. Here's how:

- Issue a short statement or Instagram post to clarify or acknowledge.
- Share a behind-the-scenes explanation in a newsletter or blog.
- Record a video update to show authenticity and transparency.

Remember: Proactive beats reactive. Regularly showing up with purpose, clarity, and intention builds goodwill, so when things *do* go sideways, your audience gives you the benefit of the doubt.

What to Do If the Media Misquotes You

Ugh. It happens. You give a thoughtful, nuanced quote . . . and it ends up chopped or twisted.

First, take a breath. Then assess: Is the misquote damaging or just off?

If it's minor or harmless, move on. But if it's misleading, here's how to handle it:

1. Reach out to the writer, politely. "Hello [Reporter Name], thank you for including me in your story. I noticed a small error I wanted to flag . . ."
2. Request a correction, not a confrontation. Most media outlets will update online articles if you ask respectfully.
3. Clarify on your own platforms. "Grateful to be featured in [Outlet]! One quick note: My full answer was slightly different; here's the context . . ."

Never blast the journalist publicly. Burning bridges in media is a bad look (and almost never worth it).

Crisis Versus Criticism: Know the Difference

Let's set the record straight:

Criticism is someone disliking your approach. A crisis is something that puts your credibility, safety, or business at serious risk.

You don't need a 10-person PR team to survive a social comment. But if you're dealing with accusations, product recalls, legal threats, or public safety concerns, you need expert support and a clear action plan.

When in doubt, ask yourself:

- *Will this issue still matter in 30 days?*
- *Does this affect customer trust?*
- *Could this spiral into a larger story?*

If the answer is yes, bring in a PR pro. This book is good, but it can't negotiate a legal statement or draft a brand-wide holding message for you.

Sample "Calm but Firm" Responses

Here are some plug-and-play statements to keep in your back pocket:

For misquotes: "Thanks for the mention in [Outlet]! One quick clarification: My full quote was slightly different. Here's the full context for those curious."

For critiques that sting but hold truth: "We hear you. This wasn't our intention, and we're taking a hard look at how we can do better moving forward."

For total nonsense: "We've seen some misinformation making the rounds. To be clear: [Insert true statement]."

For a public apology: "We missed the mark. We're sorry. And we're taking action. Here's what that looks like: [Brief next steps]."

Pro tip: Public apologies only hold water when you're sincere and actually follow up said apology by taking action.

Brands That Got Burned and Bounced Back

Spanx: Listening, Adjusting, and Owning It Gracefully

The Situation: Spanx faced public criticism early on from consumers and body image advocates for limited size ranges that didn't fully reflect the brand's empowering messaging.

The Response: Founder Sara Blakely didn't get defensive. Instead, she took the feedback seriously. Spanx quietly expanded its size ranges, revamped language in its marketing, and began featuring a broader diversity of models in campaigns.

Why It Worked: There was no dramatic apology tour—just visible, values-aligned action. Blakely's reputation as a responsive, human-first founder helped Spanx weather critique with grace and actually come out stronger.

Takeaway: You don't always need a press release. Sometimes, listening and evolving *is* the statement. Let your actions speak.

Peloton: Crisis Missteps and the Long Climb Back

The Situation: Peloton stumbled into PR controversy with its 2019 holiday ad depicting a woman documenting her fitness journey after receiving a Peloton bike from her husband. The internet called it tone-deaf, sexist, and dystopian.

The Response: Peloton initially doubled down, insisting critics misunderstood the ad. The brand was slow to acknowledge the backlash, and the narrative ran away from them. Stock dropped. Memes exploded.

What They Eventually Did: Peloton recovered by pivoting fast. They focused on user-generated content, spotlighted real member stories, and leaned into humor and transparency in future ads. They also invested in positive press around their pandemic boom, which changed the narrative.

Why It Worked (Eventually): Once Peloton stopped explaining and started *listening*, their marketing got sharper, more grounded, and more reflective of their actual community.

Takeaway: Don't let your ego write the press release. If your audience says it missed the mark, believe them and shift quickly.

Patagonia: Embracing Controversy to Amplify Purpose

The Situation: Patagonia has never shied away from bold political statements, whether suing the Trump administration over national monument rollbacks or publishing ads that read "Don't Buy This Jacket."

The Response: Criticism rolled in from both sides. Some accused Patagonia of performative activism. Others boycotted the brand outright. But Patagonia stayed the course, with well-documented receipts to back every move.

Why It Worked: Patagonia wasn't trying to please everyone. Their clarity of mission—and commitment to action beyond marketing—meant that controversy *actually reinforced* their brand identity.

Takeaway: You don't need everyone to agree with you. You need to be consistent, values-driven, and ready to stand behind your words with action.

Remember, even if things get messy, even if they don't go as planned, if you keep showing up, you're already winning. Your story is still worth telling.

Publicity Practice

Reputation management isn't about spin, it's about staying present, prepared, and professional. Start a Notes app doc or Google Drive folder where you can collect example responses you admire. Jot down your own go-to language. Create a cheat sheet that keeps you steady, even when things feel stormy.

Pitchworthy Power Move

Draft three versions of a response statement now:

1. One for a misquote
2. One for a minor mistake
3. One for total nonsense

This way, should you need any of the above, you're not scrambling later.

PR Myth to Ditch

"If you just ignore it, it'll go away."

Maybe. But more often, it festers. A quick, professional response buys you clarity—and credibility.

Pitchworthy Prompt

What's your go-to message if someone challenges your work publicly?

Write it. Refine it. Then memorize it.

Conclusion: The Spotlight Is Yours

Well, look at you! You made it to the end of *Pitchworthy*.

Hopefully, you're not just feeling smarter about PR, but bolder, clearer, and more willing to claim your place in the spotlight.

If you've been nodding along thinking, *Yes, I've got the goods. I'm just not sure how to tell the world*, you're not alone.

The truth is, most brilliant people don't have a visibility problem. They have a confidence problem.

They wait for permission. For proof. For someone else to say, "Yes, you're worthy of attention."

But let me be very clear: That someone is you.

You don't need a blue check to be newsworthy.

You don't need a million followers to be credible.

You don't need a fancy publicist to get media attention. (Although, hey, I happen to know a good one.)

What you need is the willingness to tell your story, the clarity to know what matters, and the courage to say, "I'm ready to be seen."

You've now got the roadmap.

You've learned how to:

- Create pitch-perfect messaging
- Uncover the right angles for your expertise
- Build a brand newsroom and media kit that screams "professional"
- Promote your wins like a seasoned PR pro
- Handle rejection, crickets, or criticism without letting it crush you

Most importantly, you've learned how to think like a publicist—strategically, consistently, and unapologetically.

This book isn't about teaching you how to chase attention. It's about helping you become someone worth paying attention to and knowing exactly how to show up when the spotlight hits.

So now what?

Start pitching. Start showing up. Start speaking louder about what you believe in.

Because no one else is coming to claim your crown. It's been yours all along.

Here's to being Pitchworthy! I'll see you in the headlines.

With admiration and absolutely zero apologies,

—KJ

P.S. Need help turning these pages into a plan? Head to hearsaypr.com to work with me personally. Or DM me on Instagram at @kjblattenbauer to keep me updated on your progress.

Review Inquiry

Hey, it's KJ.

If this book gave you clarity, strategy, or even just a sly smile along the way, I'd love your help spreading the word. Reviews aren't just vanity, they're visibility. When you leave one, it tells bookstores and algorithms, "This book matters. Push it further."

So here's the favor: Take a minute to drop a quick rating (and if you're feeling generous, a sentence or two) wherever you purchased the book. Bonus points if you snap a photo of yourself with it—those reviews tend to stick even better.

Your words don't just help me. They help the next founder, creative, or expert who's ready to step into the spotlight and needs this playbook in their hands.

Thanks for being part of this with me.

—KJ

Will You Share the Love?

If this book helped you sharpen your message or see PR differently, imagine what it could do for your team, colleagues, or that friend who's one pitch away from a breakthrough.

Pass it on! Gift a copy, or better yet, equip your whole crew. Bulk discounts are available for teams and organizations ready to get Pitchworthy together. Just reach out at hello@hearsaypr.com or www.hearsaypr.com.

Because visibility isn't a solo sport, it's contagious.

Bring KJ to Your Stage

Looking for a speaker who cuts through the noise with clarity, strategy, and stories that stick? KJ Blattenbauer delivers high-impact keynotes, workshops, and trainings designed to move audiences from invisible to in-demand.

She accepts a select number of speaking and coaching engagements each year. To explore bringing KJ's message to your organization, email hello@hearsaypr.com or visit www.hearsaypr.com.

About the Author

KJ Blattenbauer is a powerhouse publicist who transforms overlooked experts into headline news. With nearly three decades of experience helping creative founders, entrepreneurs, and industry leaders earn consistent media coverage, KJ is the go-to pro when you're tired of being ignored and ready to own the spotlight.

Her clients have been featured everywhere from *Forbes* to *Architectural Digest*, and her own work has landed in top-tier outlets across business, lifestyle, and design.

Known for her bold, approachable style, KJ cuts through the PR fluff to deliver strategies that actually work—building authority, credibility, and revenue without burnout. Whether she's keynoting a conference, hosting a workshop, or appearing on a podcast, audiences leave with a clear roadmap and the confidence to act on her advice immediately.

KJ's mission is simple: to help cool people and bold brands stop playing small, start owning their authority, and finally act like the big deal they already are. To learn more about KJ, visit hearsaypr.com or follow her on Instagram at @kjblattenbauer.

www.ingramcontent.com/pod-product-compliance
Lightning Source LLC
Chambersburg PA
CBHW071416210326

41597CB00020B/3526